VISUAL STUDIO 2019 C#.NET CREATING REPORTS

Fixed the issue with the ReportViewer not showing on the form!

Richard Edwards

INTRODUCTION

If it isn't broken, it is boring

That sounded smarter in my head than it looks on paper.

Okay, look. I don't plan on getting rich from this but the way I figure it, you shouldn't have to wait for a fix from Microsoft if it isn't coming.

The complaint about the ReportViewer control being broken in Visual Studio 2017 remains broken in 2019. And I can well understand why. First, it can't be fixed without a complete rewrite of the control. Two, its more mature older brother, the Report for SQL Server – the Report.rdl file – sells SQL Server. Three, very few people use the Report Viewer, so why bother.

Well, me being me, I love fixing issues. Especially when I can upgrade the same reportviewer from Visual Studio 2010 into Visual Studio 2019 and it works perfectly fine...almost.

As it turns out, after you've added the ReportViewer control to the form, open the form's designer and add this:

```
this.Controls.Add(this.reportViewer1);
```

right after the this.Text =

Right now, the form looks like this:

```
//
// Form1
//
this.AutoScaleDimensions = new
System.Drawing.SizeF(8F, 16F);
```

```
            this.AutoScaleMode =
System.Windows.Forms.AutoScaleMode.Font;
            this.ClientSize = new System.Drawing.Size(800, 450);
            this.Name = "Form1";
            this.Text = "Form1";

            this.Load += new
System.EventHandler(this.Form1_Load);
            this.ResumeLayout(false);
```

You want it to look like this:

```
            //
            // Form1
            //
            this.AutoScaleDimensions = new
System.Drawing.SizeF(8F, 16F);
            this.AutoScaleMode =
System.Windows.Forms.AutoScaleMode.Font;
            this.ClientSize = new System.Drawing.Size(800, 450);
            this.Name = "Form1";
            this.Text = "Form1";
            this.Controls.Add(this.reportViewer1);
            this.Load += new
System.EventHandler(this.Form1_Load);
            this.ResumeLayout(false);
```

And, for good measure, you can add this:

```
this.reportViewer1.Dock                                    =
System.Windows.Forms.DockStyle.Fill;
```

To This:

```
//
// reportViewer1
//
this.reportViewer1.Location = new System.Drawing.Point(0, 0);
this.reportViewer1.Name = "ReportViewer";
this.reportViewer1.Size = new System.Drawing.Size(396, 246);
this.reportViewer1.TabIndex = 0;
```

So, it looks like this:

```
//
// reportViewer1
//
this.reportViewer1.Dock = System.Windows.Forms.DockStyle.Fill;
this.reportViewer1.Location = new System.Drawing.Point(0, 0);
this.reportViewer1.Name = "ReportViewer";
this.reportViewer1.Size = new System.Drawing.Size(396, 246);
this.reportViewer1.TabIndex = 0;
```

But you won't get this:

Until you read my book. Btw, is that enough proof?

ABOUT ME

I have been working with and supporting Microsoft products since 1996. That was when I went to work for Microsoft and, until 2002, worked with technical support 400 of the finest technical support people I have ever worked with. My specialties included the Component Object Model, Distributed Component Object Model, database connectivity issues and the Registry. I also help support MSMQ, MAPI, and Winsock issues.

After I left in 2002, I returned in 2006 and created a content management program for the Games Group at Microsoft. In 2007, I started working with System Center products including System Center Operations Manager, System Center Configuration Manager and System Center Service Manager.

I have worked as a Consultant for McDonalds, Caterpillar, Ericson, Federal Home Loan Bank, Nuveen Investments, Rheem and United Health Care Group.

I love programming, finding and fixing issues and as a mentor during the launch of Windows XP.

So, when I saw so many people complaining on line that there was an issue with the ReportViewer, my instinctive desire to fix the problem kicked in. I should be obvious that I succeeded.

WHAT IS INSIDE THISE BOOK

There is a lot of code inside this book. My hope is to cover the subject of reporting in such a way as anyone wanting to learn how to create reports in the wide variety of ways so that anyone can use the code and learn how to produce them.

For example, the visual that I showed you was based on creating a report using registry information. It is not even database driven. That's how diversified you can go with creating reports using the rdlc reports and Visual Studio 2019.

WHAT I EXPECT FROM YOU

You have installed Visual Studio 2019, know how to create a C#.Net Windows Form application. And that is where this book will begin.

A SHORT HISTORY OF HAND HOLDING REPORTS IN VISUAL STUDIO

THE DMZ OF PROFESSIONAL PROGRAMMING

For as far back as Visual Basic 6.0, there has been this rather annoying reporting tool that you could use – and very few programmers did use – that looked something like this:

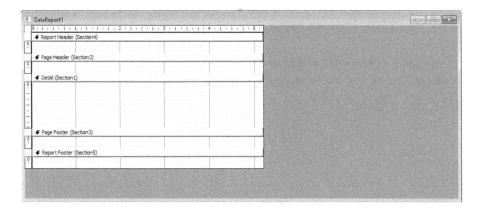

I don't know about you, but I think I'd rather learn how to drive an 18-wheeler then have to deal with trying to figure out how to use this beast.

It worked like this: Create a connection, Create A command, drag and drop the fields and add the rest of the bells and whistles that make the report look usable.

Only problem was, you had to be directly connected to the database and the table to make it work...Okay, moving right along.

XML was just coming into its own when this control came out.

In Visual Studio 2005, the last of the plain English looking XML was used inside the RDLC report files. After that, this:

```
<Textbox Name="Discontinued">
 <rd:DefaultName>Discontinued</rd:DefaultName>
 <Top>0.25in</Top>
 <Width>1.125in</Width>
 <Style>
  <PaddingLeft>2pt</PaddingLeft>
  <PaddingRight>2pt</PaddingRight>
  <PaddingTop>2pt</PaddingTop>
  <PaddingBottom>2pt</PaddingBottom>
 </Style>
 <ZIndex>9</ZIndex>
 <CanGrow>true</CanGrow>
 <Left>12.625in</Left>
 <Height>0.25in</Height>
 <Value>=First(Fields!Discontinued.Value)</Value>
</Textbox>
```

Became this:

```
<Textbox Name="Textbox2">
 <CanGrow>true</CanGrow>
  <KeepTogether>true</KeepTogether>
   <Paragraphs>
    <Paragraph>
     <TextRuns>
      <TextRun>
       <Value>Product ID</Value>
       <Style>
        <FontFamily>Tahoma</FontFamily>
        <FontSize>11pt</FontSize>
        <FontWeight>Bold</FontWeight>
        <Color>White</Color>
       </Style>
      </TextRun>
     </TextRuns>
     <Style />
    </Paragraph>
   </Paragraphs>
 <rd:DefaultName>Textbox2</rd:DefaultName>
 <Style>
  <Border>
   <Color>#7292cc</Color>
   <Style>Solid</Style>
  </Border>
  <BackgroundColor>#4c68a2</BackgroundColor>
  <PaddingLeft>2pt</PaddingLeft>
  <PaddingRight>2pt</PaddingRight>
  <PaddingTop>2pt</PaddingTop>
  <PaddingBottom>2pt</PaddingBottom>
 </Style>
</Textbox>
```

And that has pretty much staid the same ever since. So, based on that information, these report files that we use today – although cryptic looking – are a vast improvement over the first one that came out back in 1998. But they still lack the flexibility and the charm that would make them attractive for even the staunchest of die hard programmers to want to think twice about pasing up.

There is just not enough room in them for 100% flexibility and creativity in them. Almost as though programmers are working for Microsoft and Office products instead of the type of freedom and flexibility the world of programming so deperately needs. And to be honest, I've had my fill of being an electronic grease monkey.

THE *ONE-TO-MANY* ENUMERATOR CONCEPT

From database driven to XML

Every report is built on a collection of two rows of columns. The header column and the data column. The data column is the row of columns – fields – which are incremented based on the collection of rows and columns that you would normally expect to see with a bound table. This collection of rows and columns is called a DataSet.

If you've used a stylesheet with xml, you know there is a <xsl:for-each select=""> just before the table tag and <xsl:value-of Select=""/> for each data tag you add to the row of <dt></dt> data tags.

On the next page I show how all of this - for the table segment only – is designed to create the enumerator. You may not see this code in your reports, but the basic principle is the same.

```
<table>
   <tr>
     <th>FirstName</th>
   </tr>
   <xsl:for-each Select="data/students">
     <tr>
```

```
        <dt><span><xsl:value-of Select="FirstName"/></span></dt>
    </tr>
  </xsl:for-each>
</table>
```

This also sets the stage for what kinds of formatted information can be used for these reports:

```
reportViewer1.LocalReport.DataSources.Clear();
ReportDataSource DSource = new ReportDataSource("DataSet1", ds.Tables[0]);
reportViewer1.LocalReport.DataSources.Add(DSource);
```

The ds was created by populating a System.Data.DataSet. It could just as easily be a System.Data.DataTable using that, the same code above would look like this:

```
reportViewer1.LocalReport.DataSources.Clear();
ReportDataSource DSource = new ReportDataSource("DataSet1", dt);
reportViewer1.LocalReport.DataSources.Add(DSource);
```

There is also another way of doing the binding and that is through the use of Collections:

```
System.Collections.ObjectModel.ObservableCollection(Of Services) mcHammer1 = new
System.Collections.ObjectModel.ObservableCollection(Of Services);
reportViewer1.LocalReport.DataSources.Add(new
Microsoft.Reporting.WinForms.ReportDataSource("DataSet1", mcHammer1));

System.Collections.ObjectModel.Collection(Of Services) mcHammer2 new
System.Collections.ObjectModel.Collection(Of Services)
reportViewer1.LocalReport.DataSources.Add(new
Microsoft.Reporting.WinForms.ReportDataSource("DataSet1", mcHammer2));
```

The key word here is IEnumerable. Either a structure or a class is built to populate one or the other and then once filled, gets passed. Into the collection and then, that collection becomes part of the ReportDataSource.

The word DataSet1 in quotes is referencing the Report's internal DataSet name that it binds to:

```
<DataSets>
  <DataSet Name="DataSet1">
    <Fields>
```

```xml
<Field Name="ProductID">
 <DataField>ProductID</DataField>
 <rd:TypeName>System.Int32</rd:TypeName>
</Field>
<Field Name="ProductName">
 <DataField>ProductName</DataField>
 <rd:TypeName>System.String</rd:TypeName>
</Field>
<Field Name="SupplierID">
 <DataField>SupplierID</DataField>
 <rd:TypeName>System.Int32</rd:TypeName>
</Field>
<Field Name="CategoryID">
 <DataField>CategoryID</DataField>
 <rd:TypeName>System.Int32</rd:TypeName>
</Field>
<Field Name="QuantityPerUnit">
 <DataField>QuantityPerUnit</DataField>
 <rd:TypeName>System.String</rd:TypeName>
</Field>
<Field Name="UnitPrice">
 <DataField>UnitPrice</DataField>
 <rd:TypeName>System.Decimal</rd:TypeName>
</Field>
<Field Name="UnitsInStock">
 <DataField>UnitsInStock</DataField>
 <rd:TypeName>System.Int16</rd:TypeName>
</Field>
<Field Name="UnitsOnOrder">
 <DataField>UnitsOnOrder</DataField>
 <rd:TypeName>System.Int16</rd:TypeName>
</Field>
<Field Name="ReorderLevel">
 <DataField>ReorderLevel</DataField>
 <rd:TypeName>System.Int16</rd:TypeName>
</Field>
<Field Name="Discontinued">
 <DataField>Discontinued</DataField>
 <rd:TypeName>System.Boolean</rd:TypeName>
</Field>
</Fields>
<Query>
 <DataSourceName>DS1</DataSourceName>
 <CommandText>/* Local Query */</CommandText>
</Query>
<rd:DataSetInfo>
```

```
    <rd:DataSetName>DataSet1</rd:DataSetName>
    <rd:SchemaPath>c:\users\administrator\documents\visual studio
2010\Projects\WindowsApplication2\WindowsApplication2\NWINDDataSet.xsd</rd:SchemaP
ath>
    <rd:TableName>Products</rd:TableName>
    <rd:TableAdapterFillMethod>Fill</rd:TableAdapterFillMethod>
    <rd:TableAdapterGetDataMethod>GetData</rd:TableAdapterGetDataMethod>
    <rd:TableAdapterName>ProductsTableAdapter</rd:TableAdapterName>
  </rd:DataSetInfo>
 </DataSet>
```

In the next chapter, we're going to cover the various ways you can bind your data to a DataSet.

DATABASE CONNECTIVITY

How we fill the DataSet

Overall, databases don't directly connect to any type of visual reporting mechanism directly. Things like the DataGridView can be populated directly using DataSource method but how many managers want to have to install a Visual Studio Application on their machines?

Since we are focused on what we can do with the Report.rdlc file and since things like the DataSet also offers a wide variety of ways to populate it. You can use an ADODB.Recordset, Odbc, OleDb, Oracle Client and SQL Client.

In the case of the ADODB.Recordset, you simply create a new OleDbDataAdapter, create a new instance of the DataSet and then combine those to objects with the name of the table:

```
System.Data.DataSet ds = new System.Data.DataSet();
System.Data.OleDb.OleDbDataAdapter da = new System.Data.OleDb.OleDbDataAdapter();
da.Fill(ds, rs, "Products");
```

I'm actually surprised this concept still exists since I believe the real purpose of it was to help with the transition from VB6 to VB.Net. But it is still around so I decided to include it.

Below is a list of common ways programmers use the .Net framework to connect to databases:

All objects listed below require a ConnectionString and a Query to work. So, without repeating this about 5 times, I'm adding it here once:

Dim cnstr as String 'A connection string used to connect
Dim strQuery As String ' the query used to return a recordset

ADO:

ADO can't be used directly with a Visual Studio 2008 to present Report. However, the recordset can be converted by the System.Data.OleDb.OleDbDataAdapter into a DataSet or DataTable that can be used by the Report.

Connection, Command and Recordset Combination:

```
ADODB.Connection cn  = new ADODB.Connection();
ADODB.Command cmd = new ADODB.Command();
ADODB.Recordset  rs = new ADODB.Recordset();

cn.ConnectionString = cnstr;
cn.Open();

cmd.ActiveConnection = cn;
cmd.Execute(strQuery);

rs.CursorLocation = 3;
rs.Locktype = 3;
rs.Open(cmd);
```

Connection and Recordset Combination:

```
ADODB.Connection cn  = new ADODB.Connection();
ADODB.Recordset  rs = new ADODB.Recordset();

cn.ConnectionString = cnstr;
cn.Open();

rs.CursorLocation = 3;
```

```
rs.Locktype = 3;
rs.Open(strQuery);
```

Command and Recordset Combination:

```
ADODB.Command cmd = new ADODB.Command();
ADODB.Recordset  rs = new ADODB.Recordset();

cmd.ActiveConnection = cnstr;
cmd.Execute(strQuery);

rs.CursorLocation = 3;
rs.Locktype = 3;
rs.Open(cmd);
```

Recordset:

```
ADODB.Recordset  rs = new ADODB.Recordset();

rs.ActiveConnection = cn;
rs.CursorLocation = 3;
rs.Locktype = 3;
rs.Open(strQuery);
```

Just to reiterate, once the recordset is created, converting it to a DataSet looks like this:

```
System.Data.DataSet ds = new System.Data.DataSet();
System.Data.OleDb.OleDbDataAdapter da = new System.Data.OleDb.OleDbDataAdapter();
da.Fill(ds, rs, "Products");
```

Converting it to a DataTable:

```
System.Data.DataTable dt = new System.Data.DataTable();
System.Data.OleDb.OleDbDataAdapter da = new System.Data.OleDb.OleDbDataAdapter();
da.Fill(dt, rs);
dt.TableName = "Products";
```

ODBC:

Connection, Command and DataAdapter:

```
System.Data.Odbc.OdbcConnection cn = new System.Data.Odbc.OdbcConnection();
Cn. ConnectionString = cnstr;
cn.Open();
System.Data.Odbc.OdbcCommand cmd = new System.Data.Odbc.OdbcCommand()
cmd.Connection = cn;
cmd.CommndType = System.Data.CommandType.Text;
cmd.CommandText = strQuery;
Cmd.ExecuteNonQuery();

System.Data.Odbc.OdbcDataAdapter da  = new System.Data.Odbc.OdbcDataAdapter();
```

Connection and DataAdapter:

```
System.Data.Odbc.OdbcConnection cn = new System.Data.Odbc.OdbcConnection();
Cn. ConnectionString = cnstr;
cn.Open();

System.Data.Odbc.OdbcDataAdapter da  = new
System.Data.Odbc.OdbcDataAdapter(strQuery, cn);
```

Command and DataAdapter:

```
System.Data.Odbc.OdbcCommand cmd = new System.Data.Odbc.OdbcCommand();
cmd.connection = new System.Data.Odbc.OdbcConnection();
cmd.Connection.ConnectionString = cnstr;
cmd.Connection.Open();
cmd.CommndType = System.Data.CommandType.Text;
cmd.CommandText = strQuery;
Cmd.ExecuteNonQuery();

System.Data.Odbc.OdbcDataAdapter da  = new System.Data.Odbc.OdbcDataAdapter(cmd);
```

DataAdapter:

```
System.Data.Odbc.OdbcDataAdapter da  = new
System.Data.Odbc.OdbcDataAdapter(strQuery, cnstr);
```

OleDb:

Connection, Command and DataAdapter:

```
System.Data.OleDb.OleDbConnection cn = new System.Data.OleDb.OleDbConnection();
Cn. ConnectionString = cnstr;
cn.Open();
System.Data.OleDb.OleDbCommand cmd = new System.Data.OleDb.OleDbCommand()
cmd.Connection = cn;
cmd.CommndType = System.Data.CommandType.Text;
cmd.CommandText = strQuery;
Cmd.ExecuteNonQuery();

System.Data.OleDb.OleDbDataAdapter da = new System.Data.OleDb.OleDbDataAdapter();
```

Connection and DataAdapter:

```
System.Data.OleDb.OleDbConnection cn = new System.Data.OleDb.OleDbConnection();
Cn. ConnectionString = cnstr;
cn.Open();

System.Data.OleDb.OleDbDataAdapter da = new
System.Data.OleDb.OleDbDataAdapter(strQuery, cn);
```

Command and DataAdapter:

```
System.Data.OleDb.OleDbCommand cmd = new System.Data.OleDb.OleDbCommand();
cmd.connection = new System.Data.OleDb.OleDbConnection();
cmd.Connection.ConnectionString = cnstr;
cmd.Connection.Open();
cmd.CommndType = System.Data.CommandType.Text;
cmd.CommandText = strQuery;
Cmd.ExecuteNonQuery();

System.Data.OleDb.OleDbDataAdapter da = new
System.Data.OleDb.OleDbDataAdapter(cmd);
```

DataAdapter:

```
System.Data.OleDb.OleDbDataAdapter da = new
System.Data.OleDb.OleDbDataAdapter(strQuery, cnstr);
```

OracleClient:

Connection, Command and DataAdapter:

```
System.Data.OracleClient.OracleConnection cn = new
System.Data.OracleClient.OracleConnection();
Cn. ConnectionString = cnstr;
```

```
cn.Open();
System.Data.OracleClient.OracleCommand cmd = new
System.Data.OracleClient.OracleCommand()
cmd.Connection = cn;
cmd.CommndType = System.Data.CommandType.Text;
cmd.CommandText = strQuery;
Cmd.ExecuteNonQuery();

System.Data.OracleClient.OracleDataAdapter da  = new
System.Data.OracleClient.OracleDataAdapter();
```

Connection and DataAdapter:

```
System.Data.OracleClient.OracleConnection cn = new
System.Data.OracleClient.OracleConnection();
Cn. ConnectionString = cnstr;
cn.Open();

System.Data.OracleClient.OracleDataAdapter da  = new
System.Data.OracleClient.OracleDataAdapter(strQuery, cn);
```

Command and DataAdapter:

```
System.Data.OracleClient.OracleCommand cmd = new
System.Data.OracleClient.OracleCommand();
cmd.connection = new System.Data.OracleClient.OracleConnection();
cmd.Connection.ConnectionString = cnstr;
cmd.Connection.Open();
cmd.CommndType = System.Data.CommandType.Text;
cmd.CommandText = strQuery;
Cmd.ExecuteNonQuery();

System.Data.OracleClient.OracleDataAdapter da  = new
System.Data.OracleClient.OracleDataAdapter(cmd);
```

DataAdapter:

```
System.Data.OracleClient.OracleDataAdapter da  = new
System.Data.OracleClient.OracleDataAdapter(strQuery, cnstr);
```

SQLClient:

Connection, Command and DataAdapter:

```
System.Data.SqlClient.SqlConnection cn = new System.Data.SqlClient.SqlConnection();
```

```
Cn. ConnectionString = cnstr;
cn.Open();
System.Data.SqlClient.SqlCommand cmd = new System.Data.SqlClient.SqlCommand()
cmd.Connection = cn;
cmd.CommndType = System.Data.CommandType.Text;
cmd.CommandText = strQuery;
Cmd.ExecuteNonQuery();

System.Data.SqlClient.SqlDataAdapter da  = new System.Data.SqlClient.SqlDataAdapter();
```

Connection and DataAdapter:

```
System.Data.SqlClient.SqlConnection cn = new System.Data.SqlClient.SqlConnection();
Cn. ConnectionString = cnstr;
cn.Open();

System.Data.SqlClient.SqlDataAdapter da  = new
System.Data.SqlClient.SqlDataAdapter(strQuery, cn);
```

Command and DataAdapter:

```
System.Data.SqlClient.SqlCommand cmd = new System.Data.SqlClient.SqlCommand();
cmd.connection = new System.Data.SqlClient.SqlConnection();
cmd.Connection.ConnectionString = cnstr;
cmd.Connection.Open();
cmd.CommndType = System.Data.CommandType.Text;
cmd.CommandText = strQuery;
Cmd.ExecuteNonQuery();

System.Data.SqlClient.SqlDataAdapter da  = new System.Data.SqlClient.SqlDataAdapter(cmd);
```

DataAdapter:

```
System.Data.SqlClient.SqlDataAdapter da  = new
System.Data.SqlClient.SqlDataAdapter(strQuery, cnstr);
```

Since all the DataAdapters are named da and they all work the same way, here's the rest of the code:

DataSet:

```
System.Data.DataSet ds = new System.Data.DataSet();
da.Fill(ds);
```

DataTable:

```
System.Data.DataTable dt = new System.Data.DataTable();
da.Fill(dt);
```

DataView:

```
System.Data.DataTable dt = new System.Data.DataTable();
da.Fill(dt)
```

```
System.Data.DataView dv = ds.Tables[0].DefaultView;
```

Or:

```
System.Data.DataView dv = dt.DefaultView;
```

The DataSet is a collection of Tables and you will see ds.Tables[0] used quite often when programmers want the set the DataSource of data aware controls. Also, the DataReader was not including because, for he reports we're working with it really isn't useful.

There are times when being able to dynamically create DataSets and DataTables from sources you want to display in a report which can't be directly imported into a report. Things like the registry, running services, event logs, installed products and file information come quickly to mind.

These can easily be added to a DataSet by converting the information into XML or manually generated from the information directly. Suppose, for example, you wanted to pull information from the Registry. Let's say, you wanted a list of all the installed 32-bit drivers installed in ODBC. You would go to:

HKEY_LOCAL_MACHINE\SOFTWARE\WOW6432Node\ODBC\ODBCINST.INI\ODBC Drivers

There you would see:

Name	Type	Data
(Default)	REG_SZ	(value not set)
Driver da Microsoft para arquivos texto (*....	REG_SZ	Installed
Driver do Microsoft Access (*.mdb)	REG_SZ	Installed
Driver do Microsoft dBase (*.dbf)	REG_SZ	Installed
Driver do Microsoft Excel(*.xls)	REG_SZ	Installed
Driver do Microsoft Paradox (*.db)	REG_SZ	Installed
Microsoft Access Driver (*.mdb)	REG_SZ	Installed
Microsoft Access-Treiber (*.mdb)	REG_SZ	Installed
Microsoft dBase Driver (*.dbf)	REG_SZ	Installed
Microsoft dBase-Treiber (*.dbf)	REG_SZ	Installed
Microsoft Excel Driver (*.xls)	REG_SZ	Installed
Microsoft Excel-Treiber (*.xls)	REG_SZ	Installed
Microsoft FoxPro Driver (*.dbf)	REG_SZ	Installed
Microsoft ODBC Driver for Oracle	REG_SZ	Installed
Microsoft ODBC for Oracle	REG_SZ	Installed
Microsoft Paradox Driver (*.db)	REG_SZ	Installed
Microsoft Paradox-Treiber (*.db)	REG_SZ	Installed
Microsoft Text Driver (*.txt; *.csv)	REG_SZ	Installed
Microsoft Text-Treiber (*.txt; *.csv)	REG_SZ	Installed
Microsoft Visual FoxPro Driver	REG_SZ	Installed
ODBC Driver 17 for SQL Server	REG_SZ	Installed
SQL Native Client	REG_SZ	Installed
SQL Server	REG_SZ	Installed

To do this through code, you would create a new System.Data.DataTable and you would add to the name, type and data. As your columns like this:

```
using Microsoft.Win32

System.Data.DataTable  dt = new System.Data.DataTable();
dt.Columns.Add("Name");
dt.Columns.Add("Type");
dt.Columns.Add("Data");


String[] values =
Registry.LocalMachine.OpenSubKey("SOFTWARE\\WOW6432Node\\ODBC\\ODBCINST.INI\\ODBC
Drivers").GetValueNames();
    foreach (String V in values)
    {
       if (V != "")
       {
          System.Data.DataRow dr = dt.NewRow();
          dr(0) = V;
          dr(1) = "REG_SZ"'
          dr(2) =
Registry.LocalMachine.OpenSubKey("SOFTWARE\\WOW6432Node\\ODBC\\ODBCINST.INI\\ODBC
Drivers").GetValue(V);
          dt.Rows.Add(dr);
          dt.AcceptChanges();
       }
    }

System.Data.DataSet ds = new System.Data.DataSet();
ds.Tables.Add(dt);
```

```
ds.WriteXml(Application.StartupPath + "\\ODBCDrivers.xml");
ds.WriteXmlSchema(Application.StartupPath + "\\ODBCDrivers.xsd");
```

This produces the XML I need for my report and the xsd. Below is the xml:

```
<?xml version="1.0" standalone="yes"?>
<NewDataSet>
  <Table1>
   <Name>Driver da Microsoft para arquivos texto (*.txt; *.csv)</Name>
   <Type>REG_SZ</Type>
   <Data>Installed</Data>
  </Table1>
  <Table1>
   <Name>Driver do Microsoft Access (*.mdb)</Name>
   <Type>REG_SZ</Type>
   <Data>Installed</Data>
  </Table1>
  <Table1>
   <Name>Driver do Microsoft dBase (*.dbf)</Name>
   <Type>REG_SZ</Type>
   <Data>Installed</Data>
  </Table1>
  <Table1>
   <Name>Driver do Microsoft Excel(*.xls)</Name>
   <Type>REG_SZ</Type>
   <Data>Installed</Data>
  </Table1>
  <Table1>
   <Name>Driver do Microsoft Paradox (*.db )</Name>
   <Type>REG_SZ</Type>
   <Data>Installed</Data>
  </Table1>
  <Table1>
   <Name>Microsoft Access Driver (*.mdb)</Name>
   <Type>REG_SZ</Type>
   <Data>Installed</Data>
  </Table1>
  <Table1>
   <Name>Microsoft Access-Treiber (*.mdb)</Name>
   <Type>REG_SZ</Type>
   <Data>Installed</Data>
  </Table1>
  <Table1>
   <Name>Microsoft dBase Driver (*.dbf)</Name>
   <Type>REG_SZ</Type>
   <Data>Installed</Data>
  </Table1>
  <Table1>
   <Name>Microsoft dBase-Treiber (*.dbf)</Name>
   <Type>REG_SZ</Type>
   <Data>Installed</Data>
  </Table1>
```

```xml
<Table1>
 <Name>Microsoft Excel Driver (*.xls)</Name>
 <Type>REG_SZ</Type>
 <Data>Installed</Data>
</Table1>
<Table1>
 <Name>Microsoft Excel-Treiber (*.xls)</Name>
 <Type>REG_SZ</Type>
 <Data>Installed</Data>
</Table1>
<Table1>
 <Name>Microsoft ODBC for Oracle</Name>
 <Type>REG_SZ</Type>
 <Data>Installed</Data>
</Table1>
<Table1>
 <Name>Microsoft Paradox Driver (*.db )</Name>
 <Type>REG_SZ</Type>
 <Data>Installed</Data>
</Table1>
<Table1>
 <Name>Microsoft Paradox-Treiber (*.db )</Name>
 <Type>REG_SZ</Type>
 <Data>Installed</Data>
</Table1>
<Table1>
 <Name>Microsoft Text Driver (*.txt; *.csv)</Name>
 <Type>REG_SZ</Type>
 <Data>Installed</Data>
</Table1>
<Table1>
 <Name>Microsoft Text-Treiber (*.txt; *.csv)</Name>
 <Type>REG_SZ</Type>
 <Data>Installed</Data>
</Table1>
<Table1>
 <Name>SQL Server</Name>
 <Type>REG_SZ</Type>
 <Data>Installed</Data>
</Table1>
<Table1>
 <Name>ODBC Driver 17 for SQL Server</Name>
 <Type>REG_SZ</Type>
 <Data>Installed</Data>
</Table1>
<Table1>
 <Name>Microsoft ODBC Driver for Oracle</Name>
 <Type>REG_SZ</Type>
 <Data>Installed</Data>
</Table1>
<Table1>
 <Name>Microsoft Visual FoxPro Driver</Name>
 <Type>REG_SZ</Type>
```

```
  <Data>Installed</Data>
 </Table1>
 <Table1>
  <Name>Microsoft FoxPro Driver (*.dbf)</Name>
  <Type>REG__SZ</Type>
  <Data>Installed</Data>
 </Table1>
 <Table1>
  <Name>SQL Native Client</Name>
  <Type>REG__SZ</Type>
  <Data>Installed</Data>
 </Table1>
</NewDataSet>
```

The XSD:

```
<?xml version="1.0" standalone="yes"?>
<xs:schema    id="NewDataSet"    xmlns=""    xmlns:xs="http://www.w3.org/2001/XMLSchema"
xmlns:msdata="urn:schemas-microsoft-com:xml-msdata">
  <xs:element name="NewDataSet" msdata:IsDataSet="true" msdata:UseCurrentLocale="true">
   <xs:complexType>
    <xs:choice minOccurs="0" maxOccurs="unbounded">
     <xs:element name="Table1">
      <xs:complexType>
       <xs:sequence>
        <xs:element name="Name" type="xs:string" minOccurs="0" />
        <xs:element name="Type" type="xs:string" minOccurs="0" />
        <xs:element name="Data" type="xs:string" minOccurs="0" />
       </xs:sequence>
      </xs:complexType>
     </xs:element>
    </xs:choice>
   </xs:complexType>
  </xs:element>
</xs:schema>
```

Why would you want to know this?

Because it - along with the creation of a report - is the Report.

Name	Type	Data
Driver da Microsoft para arquivos texto (*.txt; *.csv)	REG_SZ	Installed
Driver do Microsoft Access (*.mdb)	REG_SZ	Installed
Driver do Microsoft dBase (*.dbf)	REG_SZ	Installed
Driver do Microsoft Excel(*.xls)	REG_SZ	Installed
Driver do Microsoft Paradox (*.db)	REG_SZ	Installed
Microsoft Access Driver (*.mdb)	REG_SZ	Installed
Microsoft Access-Treiber (*.mdb)	REG_SZ	Installed
Microsoft dBase Driver (*.dbf)	REG_SZ	Installed
Microsoft dBase-Treiber (*.dbf)	REG_SZ	Installed
Microsoft Excel Driver (*.xls)	REG_SZ	Installed
Microsoft Excel-Treiber (*.xls)	REG_SZ	Installed
Microsoft ODBC for Oracle	REG_SZ	Installed
Microsoft Paradox Driver (*.db)	REG_SZ	Installed
Microsoft Paradox-Treiber (*.db)	REG_SZ	Installed
Microsoft Text Driver (*.txt; *.csv)	REG_SZ	Installed
Microsoft Text-Treiber (*.txt; *.csv)	REG_SZ	Installed
SQL Server	REG_SZ	Installed
ODBC Driver 17 for SQL Server	REG_SZ	Installed
Microsoft ODBC Driver for Oracle	REG_SZ	Installed
Microsoft Visual FoxPro Driver	REG_SZ	Installed
Microsoft FoxPro Driver (*.dbf)	REG_SZ	Installed
SQL Native Client	REG_SZ	Installed

So, how long does it take to create one of these?

I just put a timer on a form. It is empty of any code other than the code for the timer. I'm going to run the application, create a new application and create a list of installed products. This will take a little bit longer because I have to enumerate through subkeys and then retrieve the DisplayName. Let's see how long it takes from start to finish.

Well, it took me a bit longer than what I expected. A total of 720 seconds or 12 minutes. Below is the output:

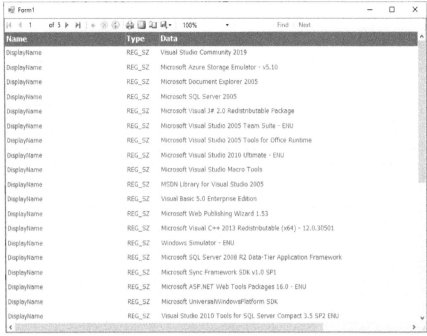

And after thinking through what I could have included the GUID and the DisplayVersion. That would make it more functional.

GUID	Display Name	Display Version
{050d4fc8-5d48-4b8f-8972-47c82c46020f}	Microsoft Visual C++ 2013 Redistributable (x64) - 12.0.30501	12.0.30501.0
{0D5009C0-F5AF-4AB1-B4F8-F334A6358CCA}	Windows Simulator - ENU	16.0.28522
{0DDCEC37-369C-484B-B16D-B4413FD42FB9}	Microsoft SQL Server 2008 R2 Data-Tier Application Framework	10.50.1447.4
{0E3DFC64-CC49-48E2-8C9C-58EF129675DB}	Microsoft Sync Framework SDK v1.0 SP1	1.0.3010.0
{110D76A4-84DA-31E8-8109-9F8D98759ABC}	Microsoft ASP.NET Web Tools Packages 16.0 - ENU	1.0.20910.0
{111EA02F-B08D-42ED-ADA5-E2A4B58815E5}	Microsoft UniversalWindowsPlatform SDK	15.9.11
{112C23F2-C036-4D40-8ED4-0CB47BF5555C}	Visual Studio 2010 Tools for SQL Server Compact 3.5 SP2 ENU	4.0.8080.0
{126dedf0-cc0e-4b48-9ece-806b0e437195}	Windows Software Development Kit - Windows 10.0.18362.1	10.1.18362.1
{12702494-9E6A-3F5E-9441-2B70258A639B}	Microsoft .NET CoreRuntime SDK	1.1.27004.0
{1282C0BC-3B22-33D4-872E-62922415DDCA}	Microsoft ReportViewer 2010 SP1 Redistributable (KB2549864)	10.0.40220
{1282C0BC-3B22-33D4-872E-62922415DDCA}.KB2293053		
{1282C0BC-3B22-33D4-872E-62922415DDCA}.KB2450801		
{1282C0BC-3B22-33D4-872E-62922415DDCA}.KB2549864		
{1309C6A4-4965-4AEC-9175-08B54A10FA48}	Microsoft SQL Server 2005 Mobile [ENU] Developer Tools	3.0.0.0
{1395207A-B7B3-F4F8-5F29-5CD18E816887}	Universal CRT Extension SDK	10.1.18362.1
{13A4EE12-23EA-3371-91EE-EFB36DDFFF3E}	Microsoft Visual C++ 2013 x86 Minimum Runtime - 12.0.21005	12.0.21005
{14DD7530-CCD2-3798-B37D-3B39ED6A441C}	Microsoft Visual Studio 2010 ADO.NET Entity Framework Tools	10.0.30319
{154EEEB2-18D9-4FD5-EDE1-6D0B318FAC53}	Windows Mobile Extension SDK Contracts	10.1.18362.1
{15E06EC7-2755-B007-45AD-9B0F1679A6BE}	Windows App Certification Kit x64	10.1.18362.1
{166BCCDD-48C1-8103-A7E7-0F3DE471223D}	Windows SDK Desktop Libs arm64	10.1.18362.1
{17B4ABCD-F7FE-47E2-A87D-1F31E7242D0D}	Microsoft .NET Framework 4.7.2 Targeting Pack	4.7.03062
{17B66E83-18C9-11D5-A54A-0090278A1B88}	Microsoft FrontPage Client - English	7.00.9209
{1803A630-3C38-402B-9B9A-0CB37243539C}	Microsoft ASP.NET MVC 2	2.0.50217.0

Here's the code that made it work:

```csharp
using Microsoft.Win32;


        string[] skeys =
Registry.LocalMachine.OpenSubKey("SOFTWARE\\WOW6432Node\\Microsoft\\Windows\Current
Version\\Uninstall").GetSubKeyNames();

        foreach (String key in skeys)
        {

          if (key.Substring(0, 0) == "{")
          {

            System.Data.DataRow dr = dt.NewRow();
            dr[0] = key;
            try
            {
              String v =
(System.String)Registry.LocalMachine.OpenSubKey("SOFTWARE\\WOW6432Node\\Microsoft\\W
indows\\CurrentVersion\\Uninstall\\" + key).GetValue("DisplayName");
              dr[1] = v;
            }
            catch (Exception ex)
            {
              dr[1] = "";
            }
            try
            {
              string w =
(System.String)Registry.LocalMachine.OpenSubKey("SOFTWARE\\WOW6432Node\\Microsoft\\W
indows\\CurrentVersion\\Uninstall\\" + key).GetValue("DisplayVersion");

              dr[2] = w;
            }
            catch (Exception ex)
            {
              dr[2] = "";
            }
            dt.Rows.Add(dr);
            dt.AcceptChanges();

          }
        }
        System.Data.DataSet ds = new System.Data.DataSet();
        ds.Tables.Add(dt);
        ds.WriteXml(Application.StartupPath + "\\InstalledProducts.xml");
        ds.WriteXmlSchema(Application.StartupPath + "\\InstalledProducts.xsd");
        }
```

The code above gets commented out or removed once the two xml files have been created. The code below gets uncommented or added and modified as necessary when the report has been created and the ReportViewer control has been added.

```
System.Data.DataSet ds = new System.Data.DataSet();

ds.ReadXml("C:\\Users\\Administrator\\source\\repos\\WindowsFormsApp5\\WindowsFormsAp
p5\\CurrentVersion.xml");
        reportViewer1.LocalReport.ReportPath =
"C:\\Users\\Administrator\\source\\repos\\WindowsFormsApp5\\WindowsFormsApp5\\Report2.r
dlc";
        reportViewer1.LocalReport.DataSources.Clear();
        reportViewer1.LocalReport.DataSources.Add(new
Microsoft.Reporting.WinForms.ReportDataSource("DataSet1", ds.Tables[0]));
        reportViewer1.RefreshReport();
```

But let's start your journey using this silly but usable xml:

```
<?xml version="1.0" encoding="iso-8859-1"?>
<data>
  <companylovesmissery>
    <onereason>You like to know you aren't alone</onereason>
    <secondreason>Someone might have a solution</secondreason>
    <thirdreason>You are comforted the world didn't end</thirdreason>
  </companylovesmissery>
</data>
```

This is as simple as element XML can get.

Will it work in a report?

By itself, no. But combine the ability of the System.Data.DataSet to produce the xml and the xsd files needed to create and populate the report. The only two things needed is the report and the report viewer control.

IT IS THE XSD THAT MAKES THE MAGIC HAPPEN

The collection of rows starts with companylovesmisery and its collection of columns is sandwiched in between. The data tag is not where the usable XML begins but after it. If memory serves me well, by xml standards the data tag is not a player in all of this because it is the root node and you are only allowed one of these in the entire body of XML. A kind of pass through junction box. Both simple attribute and element xml is what can be used in in the Report.rdlc file because it is designed to enumerate through singular node depths.

By that I mean it can use this:

```
<row>
  <col>
```

```
    <col>
    <col>
  </row>
```

It can't use:
```
 <row>
 <col>
   <col>
     <col>
   </col>
  </col>
 </row>
```

It can use:
```
<?xml version='1.0' encoding='iso-8859-1'?>
<data>
<row column1="1cone" column2="2cone" column3="3cone"/>
<row column1="1ctwo" column2="2ctwo" column3="3ctwo"/>
<row column1="1cthree" column2="2cthree" column3="3cthree"/>
<row column1="1cfour" column2="2cfour" column3="3cfour"/>
</data>
```

It can't use:
```
<row>
   <col Attribute="" Attribute="" Attribute="" Attribute="" Attribute="">value</col>
   <col Attribute="" Attribute="" Attribute="" Attribute="" Attribute="">value</col>
   <col Attribute="" Attribute="" Attribute="" Attribute="" Attribute="">value</col>
</row>
```

Now, that's not to say the XSD can't be built to use your own personal or customized variation of the xml. It is the report itself that must display the information and as far as it is concerned, the iterations of rows must have column values that match what you decided to use in your report.

Furthermore, as you will soon discover, you don't have to include all of the columns available in your report to get it to work either. I have a perfect example of this I will show you later on. Right now, we need to create the xsd file.

Giving Microsoft credit where credit is due, they sure make it easy to generate an xsd file. I need you to copy and paste the xml below into Notepad.

```
<?xml version='1.0' encoding='iso-8859-1'?>
```

```
<data>
  <row column1="1cone" column2="2cone" column3="3cone"/>
  <row column1="1ctwo" column2="2ctwo" column3="3ctwo"/>
  <row column1="1cthree" column2="2cthree" column3="3cthree"/>
  <row column1="1cfour" column2="2cfour" column3="3cfour"/>
</data>
```

Save it as Starter.xml and don't forget the double quotes around the filename otherwise Notepad will save it as a text file. You're also going to need to know where the file is now residing otherwise you can't do the next step.

Which is, create a new Visual Studio WinForms Project and call it: worker bee or whatever you want to call it. I like putting my test subjects up on my desktop where I can see them. That way they can't run away and hide.

Anyway, the code looks like this:

```
System.Data.DataSet ds = new System.Data.DataSet();
ds.ReadXml("C:\\Users\\Administrator\\Desktop\\TestFolder\\starter.xml");
ds.WriteXmlSchema("C:\\Users\\Administrator\\Desktop\\TestFolder\\starter.xsd");
```

The output looks like this:

```
<?xml version="1.0" standalone="yes"?>
<xs:schema     id="data"     xmlns=""     xmlns:xs="http://www.w3.org/2001/XMLSchema"
xmlns:msdata="urn:schemas-microsoft-com:xml-msdata">
  <xs:element name="data" msdata:IsDataSet="true" msdata:UseCurrentLocale="true">
    <xs:complexType>
      <xs:choice minOccurs="0" maxOccurs="unbounded">
        <xs:element name="row">
          <xs:complexType>
            <xs:attribute name="column1" type="xs:string" />
            <xs:attribute name="column2" type="xs:string" />
            <xs:attribute name="column3" type="xs:string" />
          </xs:complexType>
        </xs:element>
      </xs:choice>
    </xs:complexType>
  </xs:element>
</xs:schema>
```

The next step is to create a new Visual Studio 2019 C# Windows forms project and add the two files to it:

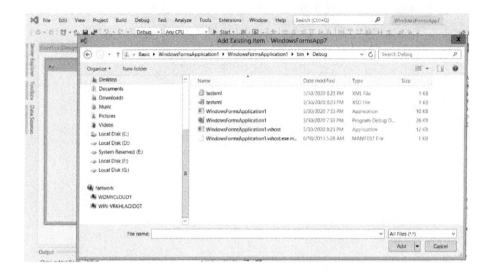

You should now see this:

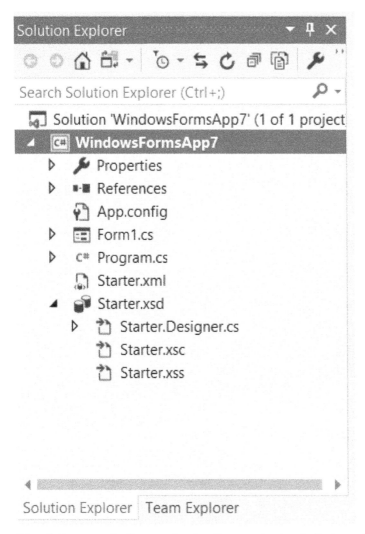

Now, let's go create the report using the report wizard. Go to project, then add new Item.

Another window will be displayed:

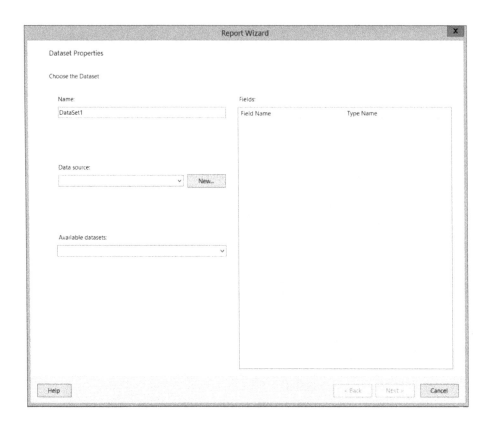

Click on the ComboBox and see if Data is already there. I should be. Select it.

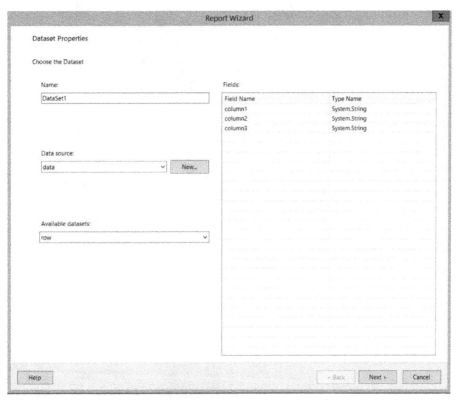

Click next. Drag and drop the three columns into the values: ListBox.

Click next. Click next. Click Finish.

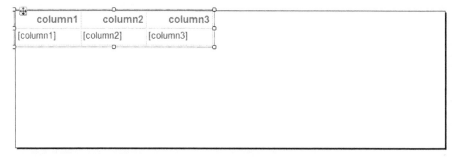

Now, we have our report but all the top columns are lined up to the right. Move the mouse to the top column1 and click on it. Move the mouse over to the right to column3 and hold down the shift button while performing a mouse click inside column3.

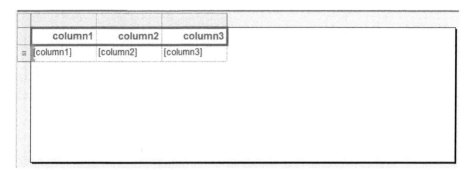

Go over to the properties and look for TextAlign and click to the right of the word right, select left from the dropdown list.:

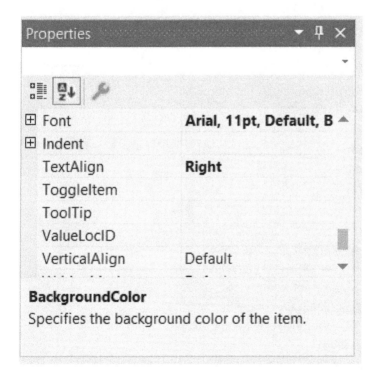

Your top columns should all be aligned to the left.

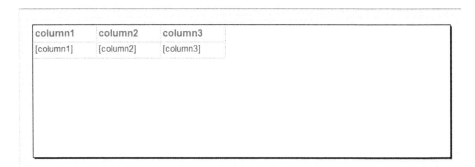

column1	column2	column3
[column1]	[column2]	[column3]

Now, let's add the report viewer. And, of course, it doesn't show up. To fix this, were going to expand the visibility of all the files as shown below:

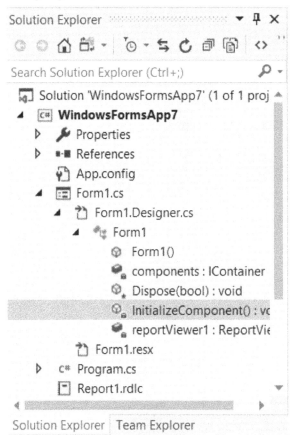

We're going to open the InitializeComponent():void file and edit it.

```
partial class Form1
{
    /// <summary>
    /// Required designer variable.
    /// </summary>
    private System.ComponentModel.IContainer components = null;

    /// <summary>
    /// Clean up any resources being used.
    /// </summary>
    /// <param name="disposing">true if managed resources should be disposed; otherwise,
false.</param>
    protected override void Dispose(bool disposing)
    {
        if (disposing && (components != null))
        {
            components.Dispose();
        }
        base.Dispose(disposing);
    }

    #region Windows Form Designer generated code

    /// <summary>
    /// Required method for Designer support - do not modify
    /// the contents of this method with the code editor.
    /// </summary>
    private void InitializeComponent()
    {
        this.reportViewer1 = new Microsoft.Reporting.WinForms.ReportViewer();
        this.SuspendLayout();
        //
        // reportViewer1
        //
        this.reportViewer1.Location = new System.Drawing.Point(0, 0);
        this.reportViewer1.Dock = System.Windows.Forms.DockStyle.Fill;
        this.reportViewer1.Name = "ReportViewer";
        this.reportViewer1.Size = new System.Drawing.Size(396, 246);
        this.reportViewer1.TabIndex = 0;
        //
        // Form1
        //
        this.AutoScaleDimensions = new System.Drawing.SizeF(8F, 16F);
        this.AutoScaleMode = System.Windows.Forms.AutoScaleMode.Font;
        this.ClientSize = new System.Drawing.Size(800, 450);
        this.Name = "Form1";
        this.Text = "Form1";
        this.Controls.Add(this.reportViewer1);
        this.ResumeLayout(false);

    }

    #endregion
```

private Microsoft.Reporting.WinForms.ReportViewer reportViewer1;

```csharp
private void InitializeComponent()
        {
            this.components = new
System.ComponentModel.Container();
            Microsoft.Reporting.WinForms.ReportDataSource
reportDataSource1 = new
Microsoft.Reporting.WinForms.ReportDataSource();
            this.reportViewer1 = new
Microsoft.Reporting.WinForms.ReportViewer();
            this.rowBindingSource = new
System.Windows.Forms.BindingSource(this.components);
            ((System.ComponentModel.ISupportInitialize)(this.rowBindingSource
)).BeginInit();
            this.SuspendLayout();
            //
            // reportViewer1
            //
            this.reportViewer1.Dock =
System.Windows.Forms.DockStyle.Fill;
            reportDataSource1.Name = "DataSet1";
            reportDataSource1.Value = this.rowBindingSource;

this.reportViewer1.LocalReport.DataSources.Add(reportDataSource1)
;
            this.reportViewer1.LocalReport.ReportEmbeddedResource
= "WindowsFormsApplication1.Report1.rdlc";
            this.reportViewer1.Location = new
System.Drawing.Point(0, 0);
            this.reportViewer1.Name = "reportViewer1";
            this.reportViewer1.Size = new
System.Drawing.Size(793, 455);
            this.reportViewer1.TabIndex = 0;
            //
            // rowBindingSource
            //
            this.rowBindingSource.DataMember = "row";
            //
            // Form1
            //
            this.AutoScaleDimensions = new
System.Drawing.SizeF(8F, 16F);
            this.AutoScaleMode =
System.Windows.Forms.AutoScaleMode.Font;
```

```
            this.ClientSize = new System.Drawing.Size(793, 455);
            this.Controls.Add(this.reportViewer1);
            this.Name = "Form1";
            this.Text = "Form1";
            this.Load += new
System.EventHandler(this.Form1_Load);

((System.ComponentModel.ISupportInitialize)(this.rowBindingSource
)).EndInit();
            this.ResumeLayout(false);

        }

        #endregion

        private Microsoft.Reporting.WinForms.ReportViewer
reportViewer1;
        private System.Windows.Forms.BindingSource
rowBindingSource;
    }
```

Once this information is added to the InitializeComponent section of the form designer, we can close the form designer and focus on adding the code to the Form_Load() event:

```
DataSet ds = new DataSet();

ds.ReadXml("C:\\Users\\Administrator\\source\\repos\\WindowsFormsApp7\\WindowsFormsApp7\\Starter.xml");

this.reportViewer1.LocalReport.ReportPath =
"C:\\Users\\Administrator\\source\\repos\\WindowsFormsApp7\\WindowsFormsApp7\\Report1.rdlc";

this.rowBindingSource.DataSource = ds;
this.reportViewer1.RefreshReport();
```

We are basically, creating a new DataSet and telling it to read the xml, telling the ReportViewer where out report is, binding the rowBindingSource.DataSource to the dataset and performing a reportViewer1.RefreshReport().

Running the application, we see:

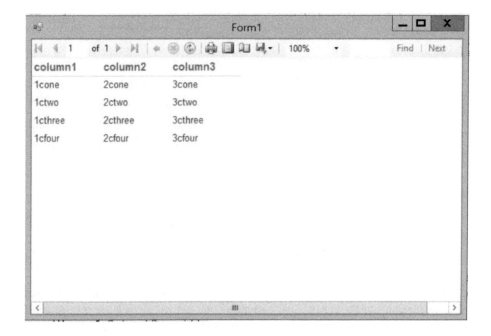

From no show to all go. That's what I'm talking about!

SOME ISSUES THAT MIGHT COME UP

Sometimes, it isn't out fault either. Especially when we go the bound data route.
Take a look:

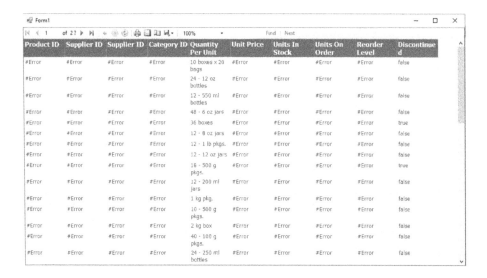

Form1

Product ID	Supplier ID	Supplier ID	Category ID	Quantity Per Unit	Unit Price	Units In Stock	Units On Order	Reorder Level	Discontinued
#Error	#Error	#Error	#Error	10 boxes x 20 bags	#Error	#Error	#Error	#Error	false
#Error	#Error	#Error	#Error	24 - 12 oz bottles	#Error	#Error	#Error	#Error	false
#Error	#Error	#Error	#Error	12 - 550 ml bottles	#Error	#Error	#Error	#Error	false
#Error	#Error	#Error	#Error	48 - 6 oz jars	#Error	#Error	#Error	#Error	false
#Error	#Error	#Error	#Error	36 boxes	#Error	#Error	#Error	#Error	true
#Error	#Error	#Error	#Error	12 - 8 oz jars	#Error	#Error	#Error	#Error	false
#Error	#Error	#Error	#Error	12 - 1 lb pkgs.	#Error	#Error	#Error	#Error	false
#Error	#Error	#Error	#Error	12 - 12 oz jars	#Error	#Error	#Error	#Error	false
#Error	#Error	#Error	#Error	18 - 500 g pkgs.	#Error	#Error	#Error	#Error	true
#Error	#Error	#Error	#Error	12 - 200 ml jars	#Error	#Error	#Error	#Error	false
#Error	#Error	#Error	#Error	1 kg pkg.	#Error	#Error	#Error	#Error	false
#Error	#Error	#Error	#Error	10 - 500 g pkgs.	#Error	#Error	#Error	#Error	false
#Error	#Error	#Error	#Error	2 kg box	#Error	#Error	#Error	#Error	false
#Error	#Error	#Error	#Error	40 - 100 g pkgs.	#Error	#Error	#Error	#Error	false
#Error	#Error	#Error	#Error	24 - 250 ml bottles	#Error	#Error	#Error	#Error	false

This one is an easy fix as long as you know what caused it. First, if you ever see this, please don't panic. It really isn't anything you did wrong. It is the wizard itself causing the issue. This: [Sum(SupplierID)] needs to be this: [SupplierID].

In-other-words, all of the number fields have to be cleaned up. You can do this by double clicking on the offending value as shown below:

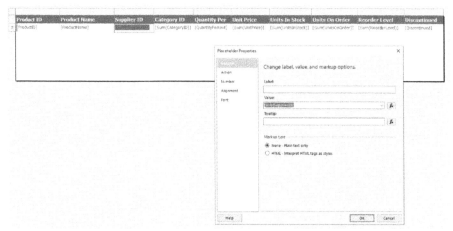

Once the fields are fixed, run the report again and you will see this:

Product ID	Product Name	Supplier ID	Category ID	Quantity Per Unit	Unit Price	Units In Stock	Units On Order	Reorder Level	Discontinued
1	Chai	1	1	10 boxes x 20 bags	18	39	0	10	false
2	Chang	1	1	24 - 12 oz bottles	19	17	40	25	false
3	Aniseed Syrup	1	2	12 - 550 ml bottles	10	13	70	25	false
4	Chef Anton's Cajun Seasoning	2	2	48 - 6 oz jars	22	53	0	0	false
5	Chef Anton's Gumbo Mix	2	2	36 boxes	21.35	0	0	0	true
6	Grandma's Boysenberry Spread	3	2	12 - 8 oz jars	25	120	0	25	false
7	Uncle Bob's Organic Dried Pears	3	7	12 - 1 lb pkgs.	30	15	0	10	false
8	Northwoods Cranberry Sauce	3	2	12 - 12 oz jars	40	6	0	0	false
9	Mishi Kobe Niku	4	6	18 - 500 g pkgs.	97	29	0	0	true
10	Ikura	4	8	12 - 200 ml jars	31	31	0	0	false
11	Queso Cabrales	5	4	1 kg pkg.	21	22	30	30	false
12	Queso Manchego La Pastora	5	4	10 - 500 g pkgs.	38	86	0	0	false
13	Konbu	6	8	2 kg box	6	24	0	5	false
14	Tofu	6	7	40 - 100 g pkgs.	23.25	35	0	0	false
15	Genen Shouyu	6	2	24 - 250 ml bottles	15.5	39	0	5	false
16	Pavlova	7	3	32 - 500 g boxes	17.45	29	0	10	false
17	Alice Mutton	7	6	20 - 1 kg tins	39	0	0	0	true
18	Carnarvon Tigers	7	8	16 kg pkg.	62.5	42	0	0	false
19	Teatime Chocolate Biscuits	8	3	10 boxes x 12 pieces	9.2	25	0	5	false
20	Sir Rodney's Marmalade	8	3	30 gift boxes	81	40	0	0	false
21	Sir Rodney's Scones	8	3	24 pkgs. x 4 pieces	10	3	40	5	false
22	Gustaf's Knäckebröd	9	5	24 - 500 g pkgs.	21	104	0	25	false

Issue resolved.

TIME TO RECAP

Let's make this interesting

First, let's talk about what we just did. We started by using a dataset. We took some imaginary XML that had one row and three columns, had the dataset read it and then export an XSD file. We then created a new Visual Studio Application in VB.Net and used the project/add existing Items to import both the xml and the xsd files into the application's Solution Explorer.

Once we did that, we went back over to Projects and then clicked on the add a new Item. That let us first select the report wizard. When then used it to create our report.

When we were finished creating the report, we then added a Report Viewer control to the form, docked the control and added in our report.

We then added some code in the Form load that set the binding to a dataset that was populated with the xml.

After running it and seeing the report work, we stopped the program, deleted Form1 added a new Form1 and proceeded through all of the steps again but this time we added an empty report and manually built the report. Following the steps that we used after the report was created, we ran the application and saw that our report worked, again, as expected.

We also fixed an issue that often occurs with numeric values.

Now, I want you to think about this for a minute.

Anything that has columns and rows can be used to create a report. Not just information from databases but from resources such as the registry, event logs, products, services, processes and files.

Heck throw in the kitchen sink while you're at it, right?

The point is, you are not limited to just database information and we just proved that, didn't we?

Well, we did with using some simple Element XML.

Let's do a report using simple Attribute XML and then working with database bound reports.

The simple attribute looks like this:

```
<?xml version='1.0' encoding='iso-8859-1'?>
<data>
<row column1="1cone" column2="2cone" column3="3cone"/>
<row column1="1ctwo" column2="2ctwo" column3="3ctwo"/>
<row column1="1cthree" column2="2cthree" column3="3cthree"/>
<row column1="1cfour" column2="2cfour" column3="3cfour"/>
</data>
```

The key thing here is to remember the DataMember will never be <data>. It will always be the next node between the <data> and the </data>. In the case of the Attribute XML format, it is the row tag that helps with the data binding process.

The trickledown effect

First, what you just worked through is exactly how this works from top to bottom. Meaning, if you try changing the report you have to make changes in the XSD and in the XML.

In-other-words from the report's perspective, it is all up stream. And that is provided that you have a strong desire to tempt fate – and the possibility of your job being on the line. Didn't we just see how the effect of using attribute xml had on the rendering and I showed you how to fix it? And that was from the very top.

Where was this fixed at?

In the form designer. So, if you didn't know that and thought everything that you had to worry about was in the XML, XSD, Report File or Report Viewer, you would have never looked inside the form designer because that would be the last place to look, right?

I think you're getting the point.

Granted that there are a lot of very good and professional report builders capable of creating all sorts of awesome looking reports, they still rely on the internal part so of these reports to remain the same.

Well they haven't been and that's another book soon to be released by me in the near and not so distant future.

Right now, my concern is with you learning how not to have to work so hard and that means you are about to learn how to automate the entire process.

AN UNDER THE KNIFE VIEW OF AN RDLC FILE

It is not as gory as it looks

There are 6 sections to an RDLC file that can be created through automation. This is the top part that usually doesn't get changed:

```
<?xml version="1.0" encoding="utf-8"?>
<Report xmlns:rd="http://schemas.microsoft.com/SQLServer/reporting/reportdesigner"
xmlns="http://schemas.microsoft.com/sqlserver/reporting/2008/01/reportdefinition">
  <DataSources>
    <DataSource Name="DS1">
     <ConnectionProperties>
      <DataProvider>System.Data.DataSet</DataProvider>
      <ConnectString>/* Local Connection */</ConnectString>
     </ConnectionProperties>
     <rd:DataSourceID>f07dabe8-d103-4c2b-b252-2d3f24a33faf</rd:DataSourceID>
    </DataSource>
  </DataSources>
    <DataSet Name="DataSet1">
     <Fields>
```

This is where you add all the field names go. One at a time. Along with their system type:

```
<Field Name="ProductName">
 <DataField>ProductName</DataField>
```

```
      <rd:TypeName>System.String</rd:TypeName>
    </Field>

  </Fields>
  <Query>
    <DataSourceName>DS1</DataSourceName>
    <CommandText>/* Local Query */</CommandText>
  </Query>
  <rd:DataSetInfo>
    <rd:DataSetName>DataSet1</rd:DataSetName>

    <rd:SchemaPath>c:\users\administrator\documents\visual studio
2010\Projects\WindowsApplication2\WindowsApplication2\NWINDDataSet.xsd</rd:SchemaPath>
      <rd:TableName>Products</rd:TableName>
      <rd:TableAdapterFillMethod>Fill</rd:TableAdapterFillMethod>
      <rd:TableAdapterGetDataMethod>GetData</rd:TableAdapterGetDataMethod>
      <rd:TableAdapterName>ProductsTableAdapter</rd:TableAdapterName>
    </rd:DataSetInfo>
  </DataSet>
 </DataSets>
 <Body>
  <ReportItems>
   <Tablix Name="Tablix1">
    <TablixBody>
     <TablixColumns>
```

If you are building this through automation and you've created the xsd after you've added the xsd to your application, you can then fill in the SchemaPath. The products in yellow is the table.

Our next group of enumerations must equal to the amount of fields you added initially and the width is the where using the DataGridView1.Row(0).Cells(x).Size Width / 65 will give you the width you need to add to each Column.

```
    <TablixColumn>
      <Width>1in</Width>
    </TablixColumn>

    </TablixColumns>
    <TablixRows>
     <TablixRow>
      <Height>0.25in</Height>
      <TablixCells>
```

The first row of the table used to display the data is for the captions. So, the textbox with a numerical number with make each unique:

```
      <TablixCell>
```

```xml
<CellContents>
  <Textbox Name="Textbox" & x>
    <CanGrow>true</CanGrow>
    <KeepTogether>true</KeepTogether>
    <Paragraphs>
      <Paragraph>
        <TextRuns>
          <TextRun>
            <Value>ProductId</Value>
            <Style>
              <FontFamily>Tahoma</FontFamily>
              <FontSize>11pt</FontSize>
              <FontWeight>Bold</FontWeight>
              <Color>White</Color>
            </Style>
          </TextRun>
        </TextRuns>
        <Style />
      </Paragraph>
    </Paragraphs>
    <rd:DefaultName>Textbox & x</rd:DefaultName>
    <Style>
      <Border>
        <Color>#7292cc</Color>
        <Style>Solid</Style>
      </Border>
      <BackgroundColor>#4c68a2</BackgroundColor>
      <PaddingLeft>2pt</PaddingLeft>
      <PaddingRight>2pt</PaddingRight>
      <PaddingTop>2pt</PaddingTop>
      <PaddingBottom>2pt</PaddingBottom>
    </Style>
  </Textbox>
</CellContents>
</TablixCell>


</TablixCells>
</TablixRow>
<TablixRow>
  <Height>0.25in</Height>
  <TablixCells>
```

This is the row of columns that binds the data and must also be equal to the ones above:

```xml
<TablixCell>
  <CellContents>
    <Textbox Name="ProductID">
      <CanGrow>true</CanGrow>
      <KeepTogether>true</KeepTogether>
```

```
<Paragraphs>
 <Paragraph>
  <TextRuns>
   <TextRun>
    <Value>Fields!ProductID.Value</Value>
    <Style>
     <FontFamily>Tahoma</FontFamily>
     <Color>#4d4d4d</Color>
    </Style>
   </TextRun>
  </TextRuns>
  <Style />
 </Paragraph>
</Paragraphs>
<rd:DefaultName>ProductID</rd:DefaultName>
<Style>
 <Border>
  <Color>#e5e5e5</Color>
  <Style>Solid</Style>
 </Border>
 <PaddingLeft>2pt</PaddingLeft>
 <PaddingRight>2pt</PaddingRight>
 <PaddingTop>2pt</PaddingTop>
 <PaddingBottom>2pt</PaddingBottom>
</Style>
       </Textbox>
      </CellContents>
     </TablixCell>

    </TablixRow>
   </TablixRows>
  </TablixBody>
  <TablixColumnHierarchy>
   <TablixMembers>
```

This is the last of the enumerators we have to do based on the number of columns we are adding to the report. Again, this has to add up to the same amount of field names.

```
    <TablixMember />
```

And that ends the automation of various sections of the Report

```
   </TablixMembers>
  </TablixColumnHierarchy>
  <TablixRowHierarchy>
   <TablixMembers>
    <TablixMember>
     <KeepWithGroup>After</KeepWithGroup>
    </TablixMember>
    <TablixMember>
     <Group Name="Details" />
```

```
      </TablixMember>
     </TablixMembers>
    </TablixRowHierarchy>
    <DataSetName>DataSet1</DataSetName>
    <Height>0.5in</Height>
    <Width>10in</Width>
    <Style>
     <Border>
      <Style>None</Style>
     </Border>
    </Style>
   </Tablix>
  </ReportItems>
  <Height>2in</Height>
  <Style />
 </Body>
 <Width>10in</Width>
 <Page>
  <LeftMargin>1in</LeftMargin>
  <RightMargin>1in</RightMargin>
  <TopMargin>1in</TopMargin>
  <BottomMargin>1in</BottomMargin>
  <Style />
 </Page>
 <rd:ReportID>0ad080c2-6cde-4bc1-9ece-cb32fe582e79</rd:ReportID>
 <rd:ReportUnitType>Inch</rd:ReportUnitType>
</Report>
```

And, at this point, the report is done.

The other kind of popular Report is, of course, the database driven report and while it follows a similar development process, the report can stand on its own.

THE DATABASE DRIVEN REPORT

Thinking inside the box

Okay, so, I've created a new project and I want to Connect To a database. So, I go to tools menu and select Connect to Database.

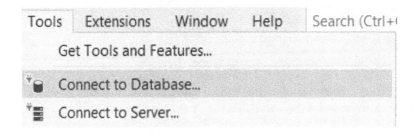

As soon as I do, I get another window:

After I click on the browse, find the NWind.mdb, I click okay. I then go over to the left of my screen and find the Server Explorer. And I see my NWind.mdb:

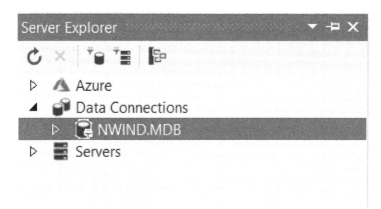

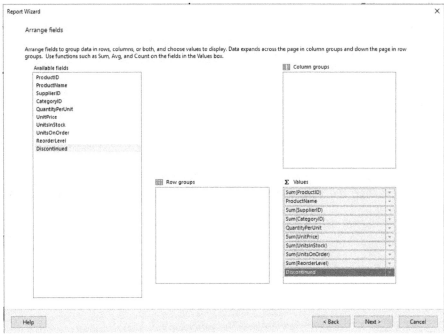

Drag and drop all the fields over to the Values listbox and click next.

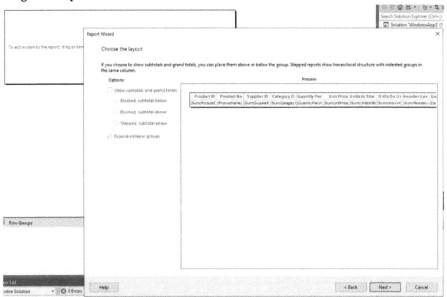

Click next and then click finish.

You should now see this:

At this point, you can highlight all the columns in the second row and at one time and change the back color and Alignment. I changed the Alignment from default to left.

THE FIX PART 1

There are actually two types of "fixes" that you need to be aware of. This one is for all of the programs we've been building that are involved with direct database access.

Reopen your form and go to the toolbox and add the ReportViewer control. Add it to the project and then, go back into the InitializeComponent(): void section of the designer. You should see this:

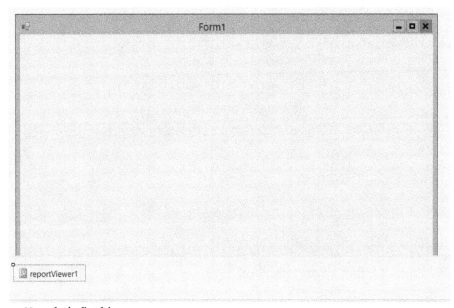

Now, let's fix this.

Click on the InitializeComponent(): void

You will see this:

```
private void InitializeComponent()
{
    this.reportViewer1 = new Microsoft.Reporting.WinForms.ReportViewer();
    this.SuspendLayout();
    //
    // reportViewer1
    //
```

```
    this.reportViewer1.Location = new System.Drawing.Point(0, 0);
    this.reportViewer1.Name = "ReportViewer";
    this.reportViewer1.Size = new System.Drawing.Size(396, 246);
    this.reportViewer1.TabIndex = 0;
    //
    // Form1
    //
    this.AutoScaleDimensions = new System.Drawing.SizeF(8F, 16F);
    this.AutoScaleMode = System.Windows.Forms.AutoScaleMode.Font;
    this.ClientSize = new System.Drawing.Size(800, 450);
    this.Name = "Form1";
    this.Text = "Form1";
    this.ResumeLayout(false);

}

#endregion

private Microsoft.Reporting.WinForms.ReportViewer reportViewer1;
}
```

What you need to be seeing is this:

```
partial class Form1
{
    /// <summary>
    /// Required designer variable.
    /// </summary>
    private System.ComponentModel.IContainer components = null;

    /// <summary>
    /// Clean up any resources being used.
    /// </summary>
    /// <param name="disposing">true if managed resources should be disposed; otherwise,
false.</param>
    protected override void Dispose(bool disposing)
    {
        if (disposing && (components != null))
        {
            components.Dispose();
        }
        base.Dispose(disposing);
    }

    #region Windows Form Designer generated code

    /// <summary>
    /// Required method for Designer support - do not modify
    /// the contents of this method with the code editor.
    /// </summary>
    private void InitializeComponent()
    {
        this.reportViewer1 = new Microsoft.Reporting.WinForms.ReportViewer();
        this.SuspendLayout();
```

```
//
// reportViewer1
//
this.reportViewer1.Location = new System.Drawing.Point(0, 0);
this.reportViewer1.Dock = System.Windows.Forms.DockStyle.Fill;
this.reportViewer1.Name = "ReportViewer";
this.reportViewer1.Size = new System.Drawing.Size(396, 246);
this.reportViewer1.TabIndex = 0;
//
// Form1
//
this.AutoScaleDimensions = new System.Drawing.SizeF(8F, 16F);
this.AutoScaleMode = System.Windows.Forms.AutoScaleMode.Font;
this.ClientSize = new System.Drawing.Size(800, 450);
this.Name = "Form1";
this.Text = "Form1";
this.Controls.Add(this.reportViewer1);
this.ResumeLayout(false);

        }

        #endregion

        private Microsoft.Reporting.WinForms.ReportViewer reportViewer1;
```

After you add the lines in yellow and close the designer, you should now see this:

But we're not out of the woods yet. The problem is the report viewer thinks it is in run mode. Meaning, in code, we have to tell the ReportViewer what to do.

In the Form_Load, we're going to tell the ReportViewer where our report is, clear all the DataSources, then build a new DataSource.

You get the report path by clicking on it and copying the path from the properties window. As for the connection, the same information that you used to create the report, the connection string and query that you used to create the report with is what you will need to use with the DataAdapter. I'm using OLEDB, but you could be using ODBC, OracleClient or the SqlClient version of it.

```
reportViewer1.LocalReport.DataSources.Clear();
reportViewer1.LocalReport.ReportPath =
"C:\\Users\\Administrator\\source\\repos\\WindowsFormsApp8\\WindowsFormsApp8\\Report1.r
dlc";
DataTable dt = new DataTable();
System.Data.OleDb.OleDbDataAdapter da = new System.Data.OleDb.OleDbDataAdapter("Select
* from Products", "Provider=Microsoft.Jet.OleDb.4.0; Data Source
=C:\\Users\\Administrator\\source\\repos\\WindowsFormsApp8\\WindowsFormsApp8\\NWIND.
MDB;");
da.Fill(dt);

reportViewer1.LocalReport.DataSources.Add(new
Microsoft.Reporting.WinForms.ReportDataSource("DataSet1", dt));
reportViewer1.LocalReport.Refresh();
reportViewer1.RefreshReport();
```

Now, run the application. In my case, I see this:

Product ID	Product Name	Supplier ID	Category ID	Quantity Per Unit	Unit Price	Units I
1	Chai	1	1	10 boxes x 20 bags	18	39
2	Chang	1	1	24 - 12 oz bottles	19	17
3	Aniseed Syrup	1	2	12 - 550 ml bottles	10	13
4	Chef Anton's Cajun Seasoning	2	2	48 - 6 oz jars	22	53
5	Chef Anton's Gumbo Mix	2	2	36 boxes	21.35	0
6	Grandma's Boysenberry Spread	3	2	12 - 8 oz jars	25	120
7	Uncle Bob's Organic Dried Pears	3	7	12 - 1 lb pkgs.	30	15
8	Northwoods Cranberry Sauce	3	2	12 - 12 oz jars	40	6
9	Mishi Kobe Niku	4	6	18 - 500 g pkgs.	97	29
10	Ikura	4	8	12 - 200 ml jars	31	31
11	Queso Cabrales	5	4	1 kg pkg.	21	22
12	Queso Manchego La Pastora	5	4	10 - 500 g pkgs.	38	86
13	Konbu	6	8	2 kg box	6	24
14	Tofu	6	7	40 - 100 g pkgs.	23.25	35
15	Genen Shouyu	6	2	24 - 250 ml bottles	15.5	39
16	Pavlova	7	3	32 - 500 g boxes	17.45	29
17	Alice Mutton	7	6	20 - 1 kg tins	39	0

And it works as expected.

Once it is created, and you've connected your report to the data source, the question that begs to be answered is: Do I really need the extra files that were created that would normally be used automatically?

Well, if you are using the database file that is added to the project, then yes. But if you aren't, both the database file adopted by the project the xsd associated with it can be deleted. But if you're wiring to the database file to create the DataSet, then you will want to use it and perhaps, delete the associated xsd file.

These decisions are entirely up to you.

USING ADO

With a little help from the OleDbDataAdapter

So, there's actually two processes here that will help you convert ADO into something we can use to generate reports. Although, to be honest, I'm really not sure if this is more me trying to keep some old ADO flames alive.

But before using MSPERSIST or the MSDAOSP providers, let's get the normal Adodb.Recordset to DataSet conversion out of the way:

```csharp
using System;
using System.Collections.Generic;
using System.ComponentModel;
using System.Data;
using System.Drawing;
using System.Linq;
using System.Text;
using System.Threading.Tasks;
using System.Windows.Forms;
using ADODB;
namespace WindowsFormsApp9
{
    public partial class Form1 : Form
    {
        public Form1()
        {
            InitializeComponent();
        }

        private void Form1_Load(object sender, EventArgs e)
        {
            string cnstr = "Provider=Microsoft.Jet.OleDb.4.0;Data Source=C:\\NWind.mdb";
            String strQuery = "Select * From Products";
            ADODB.Recordset rs = new ADODB.Recordset();
            rs.ActiveConnection = cnstr;
            rs.CursorLocation = 3;
            rs.LockType = 3;
            rs.Source = strQuery;
            rs.Open();

            System.Data.DataSet ds = new System.Data.DataSet();
            System.Data.OleDb.OleDbDataAdapter da = new
System.Data.OleDb.OleDbDataAdapter(strQuery, cnstr);
            da.Fill(ds, rs, "Products");
```

```
ds.WriteXmlSchema(Application.StartupPath + "\\Products.xsd");


        }
    }
}
```

And, of course, that produces our standard xsd we've already been using:

```xml
<?xml version="1.0" standalone="yes"?>
<xs:schema id="NewDataSet" xmlns="" xmlns:xs="http://www.w3.org/2001/XMLSchema"
xmlns:msdata="urn:schemas-microsoft-com:xml-msdata">
  <xs:element name="NewDataSet" msdata:IsDataSet="true">
    <xs:complexType>
      <xs:choice minOccurs="0" maxOccurs="unbounded">
        <xs:element name="Products">
          <xs:complexType>
            <xs:sequence>
              <xs:element name="ProductID" type="xs:int" minOccurs="0"/>
              <xs:element name="ProductName" type="xs:string" minOccurs="0"/>
              <xs:element name="SupplierID" type="xs:int" minOccurs="0"/>
              <xs:element name="CategoryID" type="xs:int" minOccurs="0"/>
              <xs:element name="QuantityPerUnit" type="xs:string" minOccurs="0"/>
              <xs:element name="UnitPrice" type="xs:decimal" minOccurs="0"/>
              <xs:element name="UnitsInStock" type="xs:short" minOccurs="0"/>
              <xs:element name="UnitsOnOrder" type="xs:short" minOccurs="0"/>
              <xs:element name="ReorderLevel" type="xs:short" minOccurs="0"/>
              <xs:element name="Discontinued" type="xs:boolean" minOccurs="0"/>
            </xs:sequence>
          </xs:complexType>
        </xs:element>
      </xs:choice>
    </xs:complexType>
  </xs:element>
</xs:schema>
```

So, we aren't really gaining anything from doing this. But there are situations where we want to pull in information from other resources such as ISAMS.

Let's do a CSV file and see if it does work.

```csharp
using System;
using System.Collections.Generic;
using System.ComponentModel;
using System.Data;
using System.Drawing;
using System.Linq;
using System.Text;
using System.Threading.Tasks;
using System.Windows.Forms;
using ADODB;
namespace WindowsFormsApp9
{
    public partial class Form1 : Form
    {
        public Form1()
        {
```

```csharp
        InitializeComponent();
    }

    private void Form1_Load(object sender, EventArgs e)
    {
        string cnstr = "Provider=Microsoft.Jet.OleDb.4.0;Extended
Properties=\"text;hdr=yes;Database=C:\\;\";";
        string strQuery = "Select * From Products.csv";

        ADODB.Recordset rs = new ADODB.Recordset();
        rs.ActiveConnection = cnstr;
        rs.CursorLocation = 3;
        rs.LockType = 3;
        rs.Source = strQuery;
        rs.Open();

        System.Data.DataSet ds = new System.Data.DataSet();
        System.Data.OleDb.OleDbDataAdapter da = new
System.Data.OleDb.OleDbDataAdapter(strQuery, cnstr);
        da.Fill(ds, rs, "Products");

        ds.WriteXmlSchema(Application.StartupPath + "\\Products.xsd");


    }
  }
}
```

I deleted the xsd before I ran this. Looks like:

```xml
<xs:schema id="NewDataSet">
<xs:element name="NewDataSet" msdata:IsDataSet="true" msdata:UseCurrentLocale="true">
<xs:complexType>
<xs:choice minOccurs="0" maxOccurs="unbounded">
<xs:element name="Products">
<xs:complexType>
<xs:sequence>
<xs:element name="ProductID" type="xs:int" minOccurs="0"/>
<xs:element name="ProductName" type="xs:string" minOccurs="0"/>
<xs:element name="SupplierID" type="xs:int" minOccurs="0"/>
<xs:element name="CategoryID" type="xs:int" minOccurs="0"/>
<xs:element name="QuantityPerUnit" type="xs:string" minOccurs="0"/>
<xs:element name="UnitPrice" type="xs:decimal" minOccurs="0"/>
<xs:element name="UnitsInStock" type="xs:short" minOccurs="0"/>
<xs:element name="UnitsOnOrder" type="xs:short" minOccurs="0"/>
<xs:element name="ReorderLevel" type="xs:short" minOccurs="0"/>
<xs:element name="Discontinued" type="xs:boolean" minOccurs="0"/>
</xs:sequence>
</xs:complexType>
</xs:element>
</xs:choice>
</xs:complexType>
</xs:element>
</xs:schema>
```

So, now we know that we can take ISAM formatted files and convert them into XSD files. But we're still going to have to convert the text-based files into usable XML. This becomes problematical for a variety of reasons.

However, some of them are also true for any older databases where tables had spaces between words and fields were limited to 12 letters.

Anyway, let's just say that you can convert the ISAMS to xsd files provided that you remove the spaces in the table and field names. Let's leave it at that.

MSPERSIST

I actually wrote my first KB article on this one and it is still around today. Anyway, the MSPERSIST provider can read a ADODB.Recordset that was saved in a XML format:

```
string cnstr = "Provider=Microsoft.Jet.OleDb.4.0;Data Source=C:\\NWind.mdb;";
string strQuery = "Select * From Products";

ADODB.Recordset rs = new ADODB.Recordset();
rs.ActiveConnection = cnstr;
rs.CursorLocation = CursorLocationEnum.adUseClient;
rs.LockType = LockTypeEnum.adLockOptimistic;
rs.Source = strQuery;
rs.Open();
rs.Save(Application.StartupPath + "\\Products.xml", PersistFormatEnum.adPersistXML);
```

This will produce the XML in the format that MSPersist can use. So, let's see if that can be used to create the xsd.

```
string cnstr = "Provider = MSPersist";
string strQuery = "C:\\Users\\Administrator\\Documents\\Visual Studio
2010\\Projects\\WindowsMSPERSIST\\WindowsMSPERSIST\\bin\\Debug\\SchemaProducts.xml";

ADODB.Recordset rs = new ADODB.Recordset();
rs.CursorLocation = CursorLocationEnum.adUseClient;
rs.LockType = LockTypeEnum.adLockOptimistic;
rs.Open(strQuery,cnstr , CursorTypeEnum.adOpenDynamic,
LockTypeEnum.adLockOptimistic, 256);


System.Data.DataSet ds = new System.Data.DataSet();
System.Data.OleDb.OleDbDataAdapter da = new
System.Data.OleDb.OleDbDataAdapter(strQuery, cnstr);
da.Fill(ds, rs, "Products");
```

ds.WriteXmlSchema(Application.StartupPath + "\\Products.xsd");

And, once again, the xsd is created in expected format without an issue. Which also means that we can use it later to bind to one of our reports. Now, it is time to look at another relatively unknown Provider.

MSDAOSP

This one works with regular XML. With one catch. There is an additional column that is tacked on to the end of the columns – or fields.

```
<?xml version="1.0" standalone="yes"?>
<xs:schema           id="NewDataSet"          xmlns=""xmlns:xs="http://www.w3.org/2001/XMLSchema"
xmlns:msdata="urn:schemas-microsoft-com:xml-msdata">
  <xs:element name="NewDataSet" msdata:IsDataSet="true" msdata:UseCurrentLocale="true">
   <xs:complexType>
    <xs:choice minOccurs="0" maxOccurs="unbounded">
     <xs:element name="Products">
      <xs:complexType>
       <xs:sequence>
        <xs:element   name="ProductID"   msdata:DataType="System.Object,   mscorlib,   Version=4.0.0.0,
Culture=neutral, PublicKeyToken=b77a5c561934e089" type="xs:anyType" minOccurs="0" />
        <xs:element   name="ProductName"   msdata:DataType="System.Object,   mscorlib,   Version=4.0.0.0,
Culture=neutral, PublicKeyToken=b77a5c561934e089" type="xs:anyType" minOccurs="0" />
        <xs:element   name="SupplierID"   msdata:DataType="System.Object,   mscorlib,   Version=4.0.0.0,
Culture=neutral, PublicKeyToken=b77a5c561934e089" type="xs:anyType" minOccurs="0" />
        <xs:element   name="CategoryID"   msdata:DataType="System.Object,   mscorlib,   Version=4.0.0.0,
Culture=neutral, PublicKeyToken=b77a5c561934e089" type="xs:anyType" minOccurs="0" />
        <xs:element   name="QuantityPerUnit"   msdata:DataType="System.Object,   mscorlib,   Version=4.0.0.0,
Culture=neutral, PublicKeyToken=b77a5c561934e089" type="xs:anyType" minOccurs="0" />
        <xs:element    name="UnitPrice"    msdata:DataType="System.Object,    mscorlib,    Version=4.0.0.0,
Culture=neutral, PublicKeyToken=b77a5c561934e089" type="xs:anyType" minOccurs="0" />
        <xs:element   name="UnitsInStock"   msdata:DataType="System.Object,   mscorlib,   Version=4.0.0.0,
Culture=neutral, PublicKeyToken=b77a5c561934e089" type="xs:anyType" minOccurs="0" />
        <xs:element   name="UnitsOnOrder"   msdata:DataType="System.Object,   mscorlib,   Version=4.0.0.0,
Culture=neutral, PublicKeyToken=b77a5c561934e089" type="xs:anyType" minOccurs="0" />
        <xs:element   name="ReorderLevel"   msdata:DataType="System.Object,   mscorlib,   Version=4.0.0.0,
Culture=neutral, PublicKeyToken=b77a5c561934e089" type="xs:anyType" minOccurs="0" />
        <xs:element   name="Discontinued"   msdata:DataType="System.Object,   mscorlib,   Version=4.0.0.0,
Culture=neutral, PublicKeyToken=b77a5c561934e089" type="xs:anyType" minOccurs="0" />
        <xs:element   name="_x0024_Text"   msdata:DataType="System.Object,   mscorlib,   Version=4.0.0.0,
Culture=neutral, PublicKeyToken=b77a5c561934e089" type="xs:anyType" minOccurs="0" />
       </xs:sequence>
      </xs:complexType>
     </xs:element>
    </xs:choice>
   </xs:complexType>
  </xs:element>
```

```
</xs:schema>
```

```
<xs:element  name="__x0024_Text"  msdata:DataType="System.Object,  mscorlib,  Version=4.0.0.0,
Culture=neutral, PublicKeyToken=b77a5c561934e089" type="xs:anyType" minOccurs="0" />
```

If we want to use this XSD to create our RDL table with it, we adding it to our Program. After going through the usual steps to create the RDL file and using the code below:

```
string cnstr = "Provider=MSDAOSP;Data Source=MSXML2.DSOControl";
string strQuery = "file:///C:/Products.xml";

ADODB.Recordset rs = new ADODB.Recordset();
rs.CursorLocation = CursorLocationEnum.adUseClient;
rs.LockType = LockTypeEnum.adLockOptimistic;
rs.Open(strQuery);


System.Data.DataSet ds = new System.Data.DataSet();
System.Data.OleDb.OleDbDataAdapter da = new
System.Data.OleDb.OleDbDataAdapter(strQuery, cnstr);
    da.Fill(ds, rs, "Products");

ds.WriteXmlSchema(Application.StartupPath + "\\Products.xsd");
NewDataSetBindingSource.DataSource = ds;
ReportViewer1.RefreshReport();
```

Here is the results.

Product ID	Product Name	Supplier ID	Category ID	Quantity Per Unit	Unit Price	Units In Stock	Units On Order	Reorder Level	Discontinued
2	Chang	1	1	24 - 12 oz bottles	19	17	40	25	False
3	Aniseed Syrup	1	2	12 - 550 ml bottles	10	13	70	25	False
4	Chef Anton's Cajun Seasoning	2	2	48 - 6 oz jars	22	53	0	0	False
5	Chef Anton's Gumbo Mix	2	2	36 boxes	21.35	0	0	0	True
6	Grandma's Boysenberry Spread	3	2	12 - 8 oz jars	25	120	0	25	False
7	Uncle Bob's Organic Dried Pears	3	7	12 - 1 lb pkgs.	30	15	0	10	False
8	Northwoods Cranberry Sauce	3	2	12 - 12 oz jars	40	6	0	0	False
9	Mishi Kobe Niku	4	6	18 - 500 g pkgs.	97	29	0	0	True
10	Ikura	4	8	12 - 200 ml Jars	31	31	0	0	False
10	Ikura	4	8	12 - 200 ml Jars	31	31	0	0	False
11	Queso Cabrales	5	4	1 kg pkg.	21	22	30	30	False
12	Queso Manchego La Pastora	5	4	10 - 500 g pkgs.	38	86	0	0	False
13	Konbu	6	8	2 kg box	6	24	0	5	False
14	Tofu	6	7	40 - 100 g pkgs.	23.25	35	0	0	False
15	Genen Shouyu	6	2	24 - 250 ml bottles	15.5	39	0	5	False
16	Pavlova	7	3	32 - 500 g boxes	17.45	29	0	10	False
17	Alice Mutton	7	6	20 - 1 kg tins	39	0	0	0	True
18	Carnarvon Tigers	7	8	16 kg pkg.	62.5	42	0	0	False
19	Teatime Chocolate Biscuits	8	3	10 boxes x 12 pieces	9.2	25	0	5	False
20	Sir Rodney's Marmalade	8	3	30 gift boxes	81	40	0	0	False
21	Sir Rodney's Scones	8	3	24 pkgs. x 4 pieces	10	3	40	5	False

LET'S GET CREATIVE!

Reports don't have to be just for database information

The next four chapters are examples of how to use your reports with Event Logs, Registry Entries, FileSystemObject and WbemScripting.

For each, I have tried to create a template based application which creates the xml, xsd and report.rdlc files in harmony with each other so that with a couple of tweaks here and there, the code can easily be modified to create additional files specifically designed to produce hundreds of additional reports from each one.

CREATING REPORTS USING REGISTRY INFORMATION

Code that creates the files for the report.

This code includes a dataGridView and the code that creates the xml, xsd and report.rdlc file.

```
using System;
using System.Collections.Generic;
using System.ComponentModel;
using System.Data;
using System.Drawing;
using System.Linq;
using System.Text;
using System.Threading.Tasks;
using System.Windows.Forms;
using Scripting;
using Microsoft.Win32;
namespace WindowsFormsApp15
{
    public partial class Form1 : Form
    {
        public Form1()
        {
            InitializeComponent();
        }
        System.Data.DataSet ds = new System.Data.DataSet();
```

```csharp
            System.Data.DataTable dt = new System.Data.DataTable();
            private void Form1_Load(object sender, EventArgs e)
            {
                ds.Tables.Add(dt);
                ds.Tables[0].Columns.Add("Name");
                ds.Tables[0].Columns.Add("Type");
                ds.Tables[0].Columns.Add("Data");
                RegistryKey                          regkey                          =
Registry.LocalMachine.OpenSubKey("System\\CurrentControlSet\\Control\\Session Manager");
                Do_Reg_Values(regkey);

                dataGridView1.DataSource = ds.Tables[0];

                string[] Names = new string[3];

                Names[0] = "Name";
                Names[1] = "Type";
                Names[2] = "Data";

                int[] b = new int[3];
                b[0] = dataGridView1.Rows[0].Cells[0].Size.Width / 65;
                b[1] = dataGridView1.Rows[0].Cells[1].Size.Width / 65;
                b[2] = dataGridView1.Rows[0].Cells[2].Size.Width / 65;

                ds.WriteXml(Application.StartupPath + "\\SessionManager.xml");
                ds.WriteXmlSchema(Application.StartupPath + "\\SessionManager.xsd");
                create_Report(Names, b);


            }
            private void Do_Reg_Values(RegistryKey regkey)
            {

                String tempstr = "";
                String Value = "";
                String RegKind = "";
                String[] sValueNames = regkey.GetValueNames();

                comboBox1.Items.Clear();

                foreach (String n in sValueNames)
                {
                    comboBox1.Items.Add(n);
                }
                for (int y = 0; y < comboBox1.Items.Count; y++)
                {
```

```csharp
string n = comboBox1.Items[y].ToString();
Microsoft.Win32.RegistryValueKind rvk = regkey.GetValueKind(n);
switch (rvk)
{
    case Microsoft.Win32.RegistryValueKind.String:
        {
            RegKind = "REG_SZ";
            Value = regkey.GetValue(n).ToString();
            break;
        }
    case Microsoft.Win32.RegistryValueKind.ExpandString:
        {
            RegKind = "REG_EXPAND_SZ";
            Value = regkey.GetValue(n).ToString();
            break;
        }
    case Microsoft.Win32.RegistryValueKind.MultiString:
        {
            RegKind = "REG_MULTI_SZ";
            System.String[] tv = (System.String[])regkey.GetValue(n);
            foreach (String t in tv)
            {
                if (tempstr != "")
                {
                    tempstr = tempstr + ",";
                }
                tempstr = tempstr + t;
            }
            Value = tempstr;
            tempstr = "";
            break;
        }
    case Microsoft.Win32.RegistryValueKind.DWord:
        {
            RegKind = "REG_DWORD";
            int tv = (int)regkey.GetValue(n);
            Value = "0x" + tv.ToString("x8") + " (" + tv + ")";
            break;
        }
    case Microsoft.Win32.RegistryValueKind.QWord:
        {
            RegKind = "REG_QWORD";
            int tv = (int)regkey.GetValue(n);
            Value = "0x" + tv.ToString("x8") + " (" + tv + ")";
            break;
```

```csharp
                }
            case Microsoft.Win32.RegistryValueKind.Binary:
                {
                    RegKind = "REG_BINARY";
                    System.Byte[] tv = (System.Byte[])regkey.GetValue(n);
                    for (int x = 0; x < tv.GetLength(0); x++)
                    {
                        if (x > 0)
                        {
                            Value = Value + ",";
                        }
                        Value = Value + tv.GetValue(x).ToString();
                    }
                    break;
                }
        }
        if (n == "")
        {
            n = "(Default)";
        }
        System.Data.DataRow dr = ds.Tables[0].NewRow();
        dr[0] = n;
        dr[1] = RegKind;
        dr[2] = Value;
        ds.Tables[0].Rows.Add(dr);
    }
    ds.Tables[0].AcceptChanges();
}
private void create_Report(String[] Names, int[] L)
{
    FileSystemObject fso = new FileSystemObject();
    TextStream txtstream = fso.OpenTextFile(Application.StartupPath +
"\\SessionManager.rdlc", IOMode.ForWriting, true, Tristate.TristateUseDefault);
    txtstream.WriteLine("<?xml version=\"1.0\"?>");
    txtstream.WriteLine("<Report
xmlns:rd=\"http://schemas.microsoft.com/SQLServer/reporting/reportdesigner\"
xmlns=\"http://schemas.microsoft.com/sqlserver/reporting/2008/01/reportdefinition\">");

    txtstream.WriteLine("  <DataSources>");
    txtstream.WriteLine("   <DataSource Name=\"WindowsApplication5\">");
    txtstream.WriteLine("    <ConnectionProperties>");
    txtstream.WriteLine("     <DataProvider>System.Data.DataSet</DataProvider>");
    txtstream.WriteLine("                         <ConnectString>/* Local Connection
*/</ConnectString>");
    txtstream.WriteLine("    </ConnectionProperties>");
```

```csharp
            txtstream.WriteLine("                          <rd:DataSourceID>4ada475a-519d-4774-8a8e-
cd804357bc15</rd:DataSourceID>");
            txtstream.WriteLine("    </DataSource>");
            txtstream.WriteLine("  </DataSources>");
            txtstream.WriteLine("  <DataSets>");
            txtstream.WriteLine("    <DataSet Name=\"DataSet1\">");
            txtstream.WriteLine("      <Fields>");

            for (int x = 0; x < Names.GetLength(0); x++)
            {

                txtstream.WriteLine("        <Field Name=\"" + Names[x] + "\">");

                txtstream.WriteLine("          <DataField>" + Names[x] + "</DataField>");
                txtstream.WriteLine("          <rd:TypeName>System.String</rd:TypeName>");
                txtstream.WriteLine("        </Field>");

            }

            txtstream.WriteLine("      </Fields>");
            txtstream.WriteLine("      <Query>");
            txtstream.WriteLine("
<DataSourceName>WindowsApplication5</DataSourceName>");
            txtstream.WriteLine("        <CommandText>/* Local Query */</CommandText>");
            txtstream.WriteLine("      </Query>");
            txtstream.WriteLine("      <rd:DataSetInfo>");
            txtstream.WriteLine("
<rd:DataSetName>WindowsApplication5</rd:DataSetName>");
            txtstream.WriteLine("        <rd:TableName>data</rd:TableName>");
            txtstream.WriteLine("
<rd:ObjectDataSourceSelectMethod>win32_bios</rd:ObjectDataSourceSelectMethod>");
            txtstream.WriteLine("              <rd:ObjectDataSourceType>WindowsApplication5.data,
win32_bios.Designer.vb,                Version=0.0.0.0,                Culture=neutral,
PublicKeyToken=null</rd:ObjectDataSourceType>");
            txtstream.WriteLine("      </rd:DataSetInfo>");
            txtstream.WriteLine("    </DataSet>");
            txtstream.WriteLine("  </DataSets>");
            txtstream.WriteLine("  <Body>");
            txtstream.WriteLine("    <ReportItems>");
            txtstream.WriteLine("    <Tablix Name=\"Tablix1\">");
            txtstream.WriteLine("        <TablixBody>");
            txtstream.WriteLine("        <TablixColumns>");

            for (int x = 0; x < Names.GetLength(0); x++)
            {
```

```csharp
            txtstream.WriteLine("              <TablixColumn>");
            txtstream.WriteLine("                <Width>" + L[x] + "in</Width>");
            txtstream.WriteLine("              </TablixColumn>");
        }

        txtstream.WriteLine("            </TablixColumns>");
        txtstream.WriteLine("          <TablixRows>");
        txtstream.WriteLine("            <TablixRow>");
        txtstream.WriteLine("              <Height>0.25in</Height>");
        txtstream.WriteLine("              <TablixCells>");

        for (int x = 0; x < Names.GetLength(0); x++)
        {

            txtstream.WriteLine("                <TablixCell>");
            txtstream.WriteLine("                  <CellContents>");
            txtstream.WriteLine("                    <Textbox Name=\"Textbox" + x + 1 + "\">");

            txtstream.WriteLine("                      <CanGrow>true</CanGrow>");
            txtstream.WriteLine("                      <KeepTogether>true</KeepTogether>");
            txtstream.WriteLine("                      <Paragraphs>");
            txtstream.WriteLine("                       <Paragraph>");
            txtstream.WriteLine("                        <TextRuns>");
            txtstream.WriteLine("                         <TextRun>");
            txtstream.WriteLine("                          <Value>" + Names[x] + "</Value>");
            txtstream.WriteLine("                          <Style>");
            txtstream.WriteLine("                           <FontFamily>Tahoma</FontFamily>");
            txtstream.WriteLine("                           <FontSize>11pt</FontSize>");
            txtstream.WriteLine("                           <FontWeight>Bold</FontWeight>");
            txtstream.WriteLine("                           <Color>White</Color>");
            txtstream.WriteLine("                          </Style>");
            txtstream.WriteLine("                         </TextRun>");
            txtstream.WriteLine("                        </TextRuns>");
            txtstream.WriteLine("                        <Style />");
            txtstream.WriteLine("                       </Paragraph>");
            txtstream.WriteLine("                      </Paragraphs>");
            txtstream.WriteLine("                          <rd:DefaultName>Textbox" + x + 1 +
"</rd:DefaultName>");
            txtstream.WriteLine("                      <Style>");
            txtstream.WriteLine("                       <Border>");
            txtstream.WriteLine("                        <Color>#7292cc</Color>");
            txtstream.WriteLine("                        <Style>Solid</Style>");
            txtstream.WriteLine("                       </Border>");
            txtstream.WriteLine("
<BackgroundColor>#4c68a2</BackgroundColor>");
            txtstream.WriteLine("                          <PaddingLeft>2pt</PaddingLeft>");
```

```csharp
            txtstream.WriteLine("                    <PaddingRight>2pt</PaddingRight>");
            txtstream.WriteLine("                    <PaddingTop>2pt</PaddingTop>");
            txtstream.WriteLine("                    <PaddingBottom>2pt</PaddingBottom>");
            txtstream.WriteLine("                  </Style>");
            txtstream.WriteLine("                </Textbox>");
            txtstream.WriteLine("              </CellContents>");
            txtstream.WriteLine("            </TablixCell>");

        }
        txtstream.WriteLine("          </TablixCells>");
        txtstream.WriteLine("        </TablixRow>");
        txtstream.WriteLine("        <TablixRow>");
        txtstream.WriteLine("          <Height>0.25in</Height>");
        txtstream.WriteLine("          <TablixCells>");

        for (int x = 0; x < Names.GetLength(0); x++)
        {
            txtstream.WriteLine("            <TablixCell>");
            txtstream.WriteLine("             <CellContents>");
            txtstream.WriteLine("              <Textbox Name=\"" + Names[x] + "\">");

            txtstream.WriteLine("                <CanGrow>true</CanGrow>");
            txtstream.WriteLine("                <KeepTogether>true</KeepTogether>");
            txtstream.WriteLine("                <Paragraphs>");
            txtstream.WriteLine("                 <Paragraph>");
            txtstream.WriteLine("                   <TextRuns>");
            txtstream.WriteLine("                    <TextRun>");
            txtstream.WriteLine("                            <Value>=Fields!" + Names[x] +
".Value</Value>");
            txtstream.WriteLine("                     <Style>");
            txtstream.WriteLine("                      <FontFamily>Tahoma</FontFamily>");
            txtstream.WriteLine("                      <Color>#4d4d4d</Color>");
            txtstream.WriteLine("                     </Style>");
            txtstream.WriteLine("                    </TextRun>");
            txtstream.WriteLine("                   </TextRuns>");
            txtstream.WriteLine("                   <Style />");
            txtstream.WriteLine("                 </Paragraph>");
            txtstream.WriteLine("                </Paragraphs>");
            txtstream.WriteLine("                        <rd:DefaultName>" + Names[x] +
"</rd:DefaultName>");
            txtstream.WriteLine("                <Style>");
            txtstream.WriteLine("                 <Border>");
            txtstream.WriteLine("                  <Color>#e5e5e5</Color>");
            txtstream.WriteLine("                  <Style>Solid</Style>");
            txtstream.WriteLine("                 </Border>");
            txtstream.WriteLine("                 <PaddingLeft>2pt</PaddingLeft>");
```

```
        txtstream.WriteLine("                    <PaddingRight>2pt</PaddingRight>");
        txtstream.WriteLine("                    <PaddingTop>2pt</PaddingTop>");
        txtstream.WriteLine("                    <PaddingBottom>2pt</PaddingBottom>");
        txtstream.WriteLine("                  </Style>");
        txtstream.WriteLine("                </Textbox>");
        txtstream.WriteLine("              </CellContents>");
        txtstream.WriteLine("            </TablixCell>");
}
txtstream.WriteLine("          </TablixCells>");
txtstream.WriteLine("        </TablixRow>");
txtstream.WriteLine("      </TablixRows>");
txtstream.WriteLine("    </TablixBody>");
txtstream.WriteLine("    <TablixColumnHierarchy>");
txtstream.WriteLine("      <TablixMembers>");

for (int x = 0; x < Names.GetLength(0); x++)
{

    txtstream.WriteLine("          <TablixMember />");

}

txtstream.WriteLine("      </TablixMembers>");
txtstream.WriteLine("    </TablixColumnHierarchy>");
txtstream.WriteLine("    <TablixRowHierarchy>");
txtstream.WriteLine("      <TablixMembers>");
txtstream.WriteLine("        <TablixMember>");
txtstream.WriteLine("          <KeepWithGroup>After</KeepWithGroup>");
txtstream.WriteLine("        </TablixMember>");
txtstream.WriteLine("        <TablixMember>");
txtstream.WriteLine("          <Group Name=\"Details\"/>");
txtstream.WriteLine("        </TablixMember>");
txtstream.WriteLine("      </TablixMembers>");
txtstream.WriteLine("    </TablixRowHierarchy>");
txtstream.WriteLine("    <DataSetName>DataSet1</DataSetName>");
txtstream.WriteLine("    <Height>0.5in</Height>");
txtstream.WriteLine("    <Width>409.52083in</Width>");
txtstream.WriteLine("    <Style>");
txtstream.WriteLine("      <Border>");
txtstream.WriteLine("        <Style>None</Style>");
txtstream.WriteLine("      </Border>");
txtstream.WriteLine("    </Style>");
txtstream.WriteLine("  </Tablix>");
txtstream.WriteLine("  </ReportItems>");
txtstream.WriteLine("  <Height>2in</Height>");
txtstream.WriteLine("  <Style />");
```

```
            txtstream.WriteLine("  </Body>");
            txtstream.WriteLine("  <Width>409.52083in</Width>");
            txtstream.WriteLine("  <Page>");
            txtstream.WriteLine("    <LeftMargin>1in</LeftMargin>");
            txtstream.WriteLine("    <RightMargin>1in</RightMargin>");
            txtstream.WriteLine("    <TopMargin>1in</TopMargin>");
            txtstream.WriteLine("    <BottomMargin>1in</BottomMargin>");
            txtstream.WriteLine("    <Style />");
            txtstream.WriteLine("  </Page>");
            txtstream.WriteLine("                              <rd:ReportID>7fa7ad8c-6890-4152-8fce-
3e6f01fffd8c</rd:ReportID>");
            txtstream.WriteLine("  <rd:ReportUnitType>Inch</rd:ReportUnitType>");
            txtstream.WriteLine("</Report>");
            txtstream.Close();
        }
    }
}
```

Here's the view:

	Name	Type	Data
▶	AutoChk Timeout	REG_DWORD	0x0000000a (10)
	BootExecute	REG_MULTI_SZ	autocheck autochk /q /v *
	BootShell	REG_EXPAND_SZ	C:\Windows\system32\bootim.exe
	CriticalSection Timeout	REG_DWORD	0x00278d00 (2592000)
	ExcludeFromKnownDlls	REG_MULTI_SZ	
	GlobalFlag	REG_DWORD	0x00000000 (0)
	HeapDeCommitFreeBlockThreshold	REG_DWORD	0x00000000 (0)
	HeapDeCommitTotalFreeThreshold	REG_DWORD	0x00000000 (0)
	HeapSegmentCommit	REG_DWORD	0x00000000 (0)
	HeapSegmentReserve	REG_DWORD	0x00000000 (0)
	NumberOfInitialSessions	REG_DWORD	0x00000002 (2)
	ObjectDirectories	REG_MULTI_SZ	\Windows,\RPC Control
	ProcessorControl	REG_DWORD	0x00000002 (2)
	ProtectionMode	REG_DWORD	0x00000001 (1)
	ResourceTimeoutCount	REG_DWORD	0x0009e340 (648000)
	RunLevelExecute	REG_MULTI_SZ	WinInit,ServiceControlManager
	RunLevelValidate	REG_MULTI_SZ	ServiceControlManager
	SETUPEXECUTE	REG_MULTI_SZ	
*			

In our new report application, the first thing we want to do is make a reference to the Microsoft.ReportViewer.Winforms namespace.

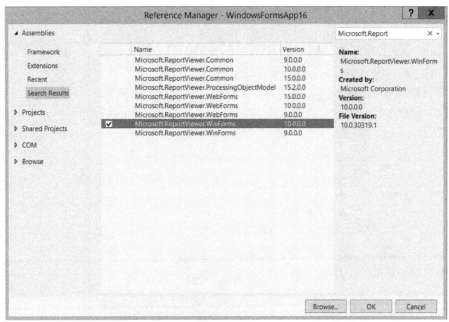

After you have highlighted the version you want to use, click OK.

Next, we want to open up the InitializeComponent: void() file:

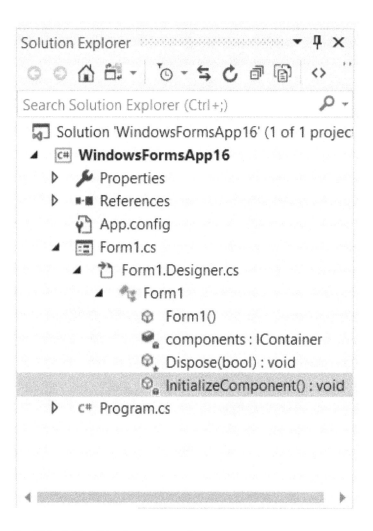

It will look like this when we are done:

```
namespace WindowsFormsApp16
{
    partial class Form1
    {
        /// <summary>
        /// Required designer variable.
        /// </summary>
        private System.ComponentModel.IContainer components = null;

        /// <summary>
        /// Clean up any resources being used.
```

```
/// </summary>
/// <param name="disposing">true if managed resources should be disposed;
otherwise, false.</param>
protected override void Dispose(bool disposing)
{
    if (disposing && (components != null))
    {
        components.Dispose();
    }
    base.Dispose(disposing);
}

#region Windows Form Designer generated code

/// <summary>
/// Required method for Designer support - do not modify
/// the contents of this method with the code editor.
/// </summary>
private void InitializeComponent()
{
    this.components = new System.ComponentModel.Container();
    this.reportViewer1 = new Microsoft.Reporting.WinForms.ReportViewer();
    this.SuspendLayout();
    //
    // reportViewer1
    //
    this.reportViewer1.Dock = System.Windows.Forms.DockStyle.Fill;
    this.reportViewer1.Location = new System.Drawing.Point(0, 0);
    this.reportViewer1.Name = "ReportViewer";
    this.reportViewer1.Size = new System.Drawing.Size(800, 450);
    this.reportViewer1.TabIndex = 0;
    //
    // Form1
    //
    this.AutoScaleDimensions = new System.Drawing.SizeF(8F, 16F);
    this.AutoScaleMode = System.Windows.Forms.AutoScaleMode.Font;
    this.ClientSize = new System.Drawing.Size(800, 450);
    this.Controls.Add(this.reportViewer1);
    this.Name = "Form1";
    this.Text = "Form1";
    this.ResumeLayout(false);
}

#endregion
private Microsoft.Reporting.WinForms.ReportViewer reportViewer1;
}
}
```

After this, we want to import our three files from the previous application:

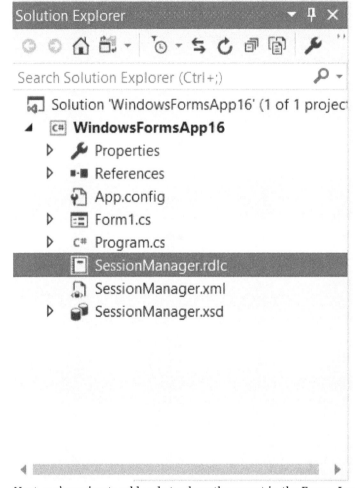

Next, we're going to add code to show the report in the Form_Load()

```
using System;
using System.Collections.Generic;
using System.ComponentModel;
using System.Data;
using System.Drawing;
using System.Linq;
using System.Text;
using System.Threading.Tasks;
using System.Windows.Forms;
```

```csharp
namespace WindowsFormsApp16
{
    public partial class Form1 : Form
    {
        public Form1()
        {
            InitializeComponent();
        }

        private void Form1_Load(object sender, EventArgs e)
        {
            System.Data.DataSet ds = new System.Data.DataSet();

ds.ReadXml("C:\\Users\\Administrator\\source\\repos\\WindowsFormsApp16\\WindowsFormsApp16\\SessionManager.xml");

            reportViewer1.LocalReport.ReportPath =
"C:\\Users\\Administrator\\source\\repos\\WindowsFormsApp16\\WindowsFormsApp16\\SessionManager.rdlc";
            reportViewer1.LocalReport.DataSources.Clear();
            reportViewer1.LocalReport.DataSources.Add(new
Microsoft.Reporting.WinForms.ReportDataSource("DataSet1", ds.Tables[0]));
            this.reportViewer1.RefreshReport();
        }
    }
}
```

And the results:

Name	Type	Data
AutoChkTimeout	REG_DWORD	0x0000000a (10)
BootExecute	REG_MULTI_SZ	autocheck autochk /q /v *
BootShell	REG_EXPAND_SZ	C:\Windows\system32\bootim.exe
CriticalSectionTimeout	REG_DWORD	0x00278d00 (2592000)
ExcludeFromKnownDlls	REG_MULTI_SZ	
GlobalFlag	REG_DWORD	0x00000000 (0)
HeapDeCommitFreeBlockThreshold	REG_DWORD	0x00000000 (0)
HeapDeCommitTotalFreeThreshold	REG_DWORD	0x00000000 (0)
HeapSegmentCommit	REG_DWORD	0x00000000 (0)
HeapSegmentReserve	REG_DWORD	0x00000000 (0)
NumberOfInitialSessions	REG_DWORD	0x00000002 (2)
ObjectDirectories	REG_MULTI_SZ	\Windows,\RPC Control
ProcessorControl	REG_DWORD	0x00000002 (2)
ProtectionMode	REG_DWORD	0x00000001 (1)
ResourceTimeoutCount	REG_DWORD	0x0009e340 (648000)
RunLevelExecute	REG_MULTI_SZ	WinInit,ServiceControlManager
RunLevelValidate	REG_MULTI_SZ	ServiceControlManager
SETUPEXECUTE	REG_MULTI_SZ	

CREATING REPORTS FROM EVENT LOGS

An easy example listing logs with records in them

```csharp
using System;
using System.Collections.Generic;
using System.ComponentModel;
using System.Data;
using System.Drawing;
using System.Linq;
using System.Text;
using System.Threading.Tasks;
using System.Windows.Forms;
using Scripting;
using WbemScripting;

namespace WindowsFormsApp17
{
    public partial class Form1 : Form
    {
        public Form1()
        {
            InitializeComponent();
        }
```

```csharp
System.Data.DataSet ds = new System.Data.DataSet();
System.Data.DataTable dt = new System.Data.DataTable();


private string GetValue(string n, SWbemObject obj)
{
    int pos = 0;
    string tn = n;
    string tempstr = obj.GetObjectText_();
    tn += " =";
    pos = tempstr.IndexOf(tn);
    if (pos > 0)
    {
        pos = pos + tn.Length;
        tempstr = tempstr.Substring(pos, tempstr.Length - pos);
        pos = tempstr.IndexOf(";");
        tempstr = tempstr.Substring(0, pos);
        tempstr = tempstr.Replace("{", "");
        tempstr = tempstr.Replace("}", "");
        tempstr = tempstr.Replace("\"", "");
        tempstr = tempstr.Trim();
        if (obj.Properties_.Item(n).CIMType ==
WbemScripting.WbemCimtypeEnum.wbemCimtypeDatetime && tempstr.Length >
14)
        {
            return ReturnDateTime(tempstr);
        }
        else
        {
            return tempstr;
        }
    }
    else
    {
        return "";
    }
}
private string ReturnDateTime(string Value)
{
```

```csharp
            return Value.Substring(4, 2) + "/" + Value.Substring(6, 2) + "/" +
Value.Substring(0, 4) + "" + Value.Substring(8, 2) + ":" + Value.Substring(10, 2) +
":" + Value.Substring(12, 2);
        }

        private void Form1_Load(object sender, EventArgs e)
        {
            int[] b = null;
            string[] Names = null;
            ds.Tables.Add(dt);
            SWbemLocator l = new SWbemLocator();
            SWbemServices svc = l.ConnectServer(".", "Root\\cimv2");
            svc.Security_.AuthenticationLevel =
WbemAuthenticationLevelEnum.wbemAuthenticationLevelPktPrivacy;
            svc.Security_.ImpersonationLevel =
WbemImpersonationLevelEnum.wbemImpersonationLevelImpersonate;
            SWbemObjectSet objs = svc.ExecQuery("Select Archive, Caption,
CreationDate, CSName, Description, Drive, Filename, InstallDate, LastAccessed,
LastModified, LogFileName, Name, NumberOfRecords, Path, Status, System,
Writeable from Win32_NTEventLogFile where NumberOfRecords != 0");
            int x = 0;
            foreach (SWbemObject obj in objs)
            {
                b = new int[obj.Properties_.Count];
                Names = new string[obj.Properties_.Count];
                foreach (SWbemProperty prop in obj.Properties_)
                {
                    ds.Tables[0].Columns.Add(prop.Name);
                    dataGridView1.Columns.Add(prop.Name, prop.Name);
                    Names[x] = prop.Name;
                    x = x + 1;

                }
                break;
            }
            x = 0;
            int y = 0;
            foreach (SWbemObject obj in objs)
            {
                dataGridView1.Rows.Add();
```

```
        DataRow dr = ds.Tables[0].NewRow();
        foreach (SWbemProperty prop in obj.Properties_)
        {
            dr[x] = GetValue(prop.Name, obj);
            dataGridView1.Rows[y].Cells[x].Value = GetValue(prop.Name, obj);
            x = x + 1;
        }
        ds.Tables[0].Rows.Add(dr);
        x = 0;
        y = y + 1;
    }
    ds.Tables[0].AcceptChanges();

    for (int a = 0; a < dataGridView1.Columns.Count; a++)
    {
        b[a] = dataGridView1.Rows[0].Cells[a].Size.Width / 70;
    }
    ds.WriteXml(Application.StartupPath + "\\EventLog.xml");
    ds.WriteXmlSchema(Application.StartupPath + "\\EventLog.xsd");
    create_Report(Names, b);


}
private void create_Report(String[] Names, int[] L)
{
    FileSystemObject fso = new FileSystemObject();
    TextStream txtstream = fso.OpenTextFile(Application.StartupPath +
"\\EventLog.rdlc", IOMode.ForWriting, true, Tristate.TristateUseDefault);
    txtstream.WriteLine("<?xml version=\"1.0\"?>");
    txtstream.WriteLine("<Report
xmlns:rd=\"http://schemas.microsoft.com/SQLServer/reporting/reportdesigner\"
xmlns=\"http://schemas.microsoft.com/sqlserver/reporting/2008/01/reportdefinitio
n\">");

    txtstream.WriteLine(" <DataSources>");
    txtstream.WriteLine("   <DataSource
Name=\"WindowsApplication5\">");
    txtstream.WriteLine("     <ConnectionProperties>");
    txtstream.WriteLine("
<DataProvider>System.Data.DataSet</DataProvider>");
```

```
            txtstream.WriteLine("       <ConnectString>/* Local Connection
*/</ConnectString>");
            txtstream.WriteLine("    </ConnectionProperties>");
            txtstream.WriteLine("    <rd:DataSourceID>4ada475a-519d-4774-8a8e-
cd804357bc15</rd:DataSourceID>");
            txtstream.WriteLine("   </DataSource>");
            txtstream.WriteLine("  </DataSources>");
            txtstream.WriteLine("  <DataSets>");
            txtstream.WriteLine("    <DataSet Name=\"DataSet1\">");
            txtstream.WriteLine("      <Fields>");

            for (int x = 0; x < Names.GetLength(0); x++)
            {

                txtstream.WriteLine("        <Field Name=\"" + Names[x] + "\">");

                txtstream.WriteLine("          <DataField>" + Names[x] +
"</DataField>");
                txtstream.WriteLine("
<rd:TypeName>System.String</rd:TypeName>");
                txtstream.WriteLine("        </Field>");

            }

            txtstream.WriteLine("      </Fields>");
            txtstream.WriteLine("      <Query>");
            txtstream.WriteLine("
<DataSourceName>WindowsApplication5</DataSourceName>");
            txtstream.WriteLine("        <CommandText>/* Local Query
*/</CommandText>");
            txtstream.WriteLine("      </Query>");
            txtstream.WriteLine("      <rd:DataSetInfo>");
            txtstream.WriteLine("
<rd:DataSetName>WindowsApplication5</rd:DataSetName>");
            txtstream.WriteLine("        <rd:TableName>data</rd:TableName>");
            txtstream.WriteLine("
<rd:ObjectDataSourceSelectMethod>win32_bios</rd:ObjectDataSourceSelectMethod
>");
            txtstream.WriteLine("
<rd:ObjectDataSourceType>WindowsApplication5.data, win32_bios.Designer.vb,
```

```
Version=0.0.0.0, Culture=neutral,
PublicKeyToken=null</rd:ObjectDataSourceType>");
            txtstream.WriteLine("      </rd:DataSetInfo>");
            txtstream.WriteLine("    </DataSet>");
            txtstream.WriteLine("  </DataSets>");
            txtstream.WriteLine("  <Body>");
            txtstream.WriteLine("    <ReportItems>");
            txtstream.WriteLine("      <Tablix Name=\"Tablix1\">");
            txtstream.WriteLine("        <TablixBody>");
            txtstream.WriteLine("          <TablixColumns>");

            for (int x = 0; x < Names.GetLength(0); x++)
            {

                txtstream.WriteLine("            <TablixColumn>");
                txtstream.WriteLine("              <Width>" + L[x] + "in</Width>");
                txtstream.WriteLine("            </TablixColumn>");

            }

            txtstream.WriteLine("          </TablixColumns>");
            txtstream.WriteLine("          <TablixRows>");
            txtstream.WriteLine("            <TablixRow>");
            txtstream.WriteLine("              <Height>0.25in</Height>");
            txtstream.WriteLine("              <TablixCells>");

            for (int x = 0; x < Names.GetLength(0); x++)
            {

                txtstream.WriteLine("                <TablixCell>");
                txtstream.WriteLine("                  <CellContents>");
                txtstream.WriteLine("                    <Textbox Name=\"Textbox" + x + 1 +
"\">");

                txtstream.WriteLine("                      <CanGrow>true</CanGrow>");
                txtstream.WriteLine("
<KeepTogether>true</KeepTogether>");
                txtstream.WriteLine("                      <Paragraphs>");
                txtstream.WriteLine("                        <Paragraph>");
                txtstream.WriteLine("                          <TextRuns>");
                txtstream.WriteLine("                            <TextRun>");
```

```csharp
                    txtstream.WriteLine("                        <Value>" + Names[x] +
"</Value>");
                    txtstream.WriteLine("                        <Style>");
                    txtstream.WriteLine("
<FontFamily>Tahoma</FontFamily>");
                    txtstream.WriteLine("                          <FontSize>11pt</FontSize>");
                    txtstream.WriteLine("
<FontWeight>Bold</FontWeight>");
                    txtstream.WriteLine("                            <Color>White</Color>");
                    txtstream.WriteLine("                          </Style>");
                    txtstream.WriteLine("                        </TextRun>");
                    txtstream.WriteLine("                      </TextRuns>");
                    txtstream.WriteLine("                      <Style />");
                    txtstream.WriteLine("                    </Paragraph>");
                    txtstream.WriteLine("                  </Paragraphs>");
                    txtstream.WriteLine("                  <rd:DefaultName>Textbox" + x + 1
+ "</rd:DefaultName>");
                    txtstream.WriteLine("                  <Style>");
                    txtstream.WriteLine("                    <Border>");
                    txtstream.WriteLine("                      <Color>#7292cc</Color>");
                    txtstream.WriteLine("                      <Style>Solid</Style>");
                    txtstream.WriteLine("                    </Border>");
                    txtstream.WriteLine("
<BackgroundColor>#4c68a2</BackgroundColor>");
                    txtstream.WriteLine("
<PaddingLeft>2pt</PaddingLeft>");
                    txtstream.WriteLine("
<PaddingRight>2pt</PaddingRight>");
                    txtstream.WriteLine("
<PaddingTop>2pt</PaddingTop>");
                    txtstream.WriteLine("
<PaddingBottom>2pt</PaddingBottom>");
                    txtstream.WriteLine("                  </Style>");
                    txtstream.WriteLine("                  </Textbox>");
                    txtstream.WriteLine("                </CellContents>");
                    txtstream.WriteLine("              </TablixCell>");

                }
                txtstream.WriteLine("            </TablixCells>");
                txtstream.WriteLine("          </TablixRow>");
```

```csharp
            txtstream.WriteLine("          <TablixRow>");
            txtstream.WriteLine("            <Height>0.25in</Height>");
            txtstream.WriteLine("            <TablixCells>");

        for (int x = 0; x < Names.GetLength(0); x++)
        {
            txtstream.WriteLine("              <TablixCell>");
            txtstream.WriteLine("                <CellContents>");
            txtstream.WriteLine("                  <Textbox Name=\"" + Names[x] +
"\">");

            txtstream.WriteLine("                    <CanGrow>true</CanGrow>");
            txtstream.WriteLine("
<KeepTogether>true</KeepTogether>");
            txtstream.WriteLine("                    <Paragraphs>");
            txtstream.WriteLine("                     <Paragraph>");
            txtstream.WriteLine("                      <TextRuns>");
            txtstream.WriteLine("                       <TextRun>");
            txtstream.WriteLine("                        <Value>=Fields!" + Names[x] +
".Value</Value>");
            txtstream.WriteLine("                        <Style>");
            txtstream.WriteLine("
<FontFamily>Tahoma</FontFamily>");
            txtstream.WriteLine("                          <Color>#4d4d4d</Color>");
            txtstream.WriteLine("                        </Style>");
            txtstream.WriteLine("                       </TextRun>");
            txtstream.WriteLine("                      </TextRuns>");
            txtstream.WriteLine("                      <Style />");
            txtstream.WriteLine("                     </Paragraph>");
            txtstream.WriteLine("                    </Paragraphs>");
            txtstream.WriteLine("                    <rd:DefaultName>" + Names[x] +
"</rd:DefaultName>");
            txtstream.WriteLine("                    <Style>");
            txtstream.WriteLine("                     <Border>");
            txtstream.WriteLine("                      <Color>#e5e5e5</Color>");
            txtstream.WriteLine("                      <Style>Solid</Style>");
            txtstream.WriteLine("                     </Border>");
            txtstream.WriteLine("
<PaddingLeft>2pt</PaddingLeft>");
```

```csharp
            txtstream.WriteLine("
<PaddingRight>2pt</PaddingRight>");
            txtstream.WriteLine("
<PaddingTop>2pt</PaddingTop>");
            txtstream.WriteLine("
<PaddingBottom>2pt</PaddingBottom>");
            txtstream.WriteLine("                    </Style>");
            txtstream.WriteLine("                   </Textbox>");
            txtstream.WriteLine("              </CellContents>");
            txtstream.WriteLine("            </TablixCell>");

        }

            txtstream.WriteLine("           </TablixCells>");
            txtstream.WriteLine("          </TablixRow>");
            txtstream.WriteLine("         </TablixRows>");
            txtstream.WriteLine("        </TablixBody>");
            txtstream.WriteLine("        <TablixColumnHierarchy>");
            txtstream.WriteLine("         <TablixMembers>");

        for (int x = 0; x < Names.GetLength(0); x++)
        {

            txtstream.WriteLine("          <TablixMember />");

        }

            txtstream.WriteLine("         </TablixMembers>");
            txtstream.WriteLine("        </TablixColumnHierarchy>");
            txtstream.WriteLine("        <TablixRowHierarchy>");
            txtstream.WriteLine("         <TablixMembers>");
            txtstream.WriteLine("          <TablixMember>");
            txtstream.WriteLine("
<KeepWithGroup>After</KeepWithGroup>");
            txtstream.WriteLine("          </TablixMember>");
            txtstream.WriteLine("          <TablixMember>");
            txtstream.WriteLine("           <Group Name=\"Details\"/>");
            txtstream.WriteLine("          </TablixMember>");
            txtstream.WriteLine("         </TablixMembers>");
            txtstream.WriteLine("        </TablixRowHierarchy>");
```

```
txtstream.WriteLine("      <DataSetName>DataSet1</DataSetName>");
txtstream.WriteLine("      <Height>0.5in</Height>");
txtstream.WriteLine("      <Width>409.52083in</Width>");
txtstream.WriteLine("      <Style>");
txtstream.WriteLine("        <Border>");
txtstream.WriteLine("          <Style>None</Style>");
txtstream.WriteLine("        </Border>");
txtstream.WriteLine("      </Style>");
txtstream.WriteLine("    </Tablix>");
txtstream.WriteLine("  </ReportItems>");
txtstream.WriteLine("  <Height>2in</Height>");
txtstream.WriteLine("  <Style />");
txtstream.WriteLine("</Body>");
txtstream.WriteLine("<Width>40in</Width>");
txtstream.WriteLine("<Page>");
txtstream.WriteLine("  <LeftMargin>1in</LeftMargin>");
txtstream.WriteLine("  <RightMargin>1in</RightMargin>");
txtstream.WriteLine("  <TopMargin>1in</TopMargin>");
txtstream.WriteLine("  <BottomMargin>1in</BottomMargin>");
txtstream.WriteLine("  <Style />");
txtstream.WriteLine("</Page>");
txtstream.WriteLine("<rd:ReportID>7fa7ad8c-6890-4152-8fce-3e6f01fffd8c</rd:ReportID>");
txtstream.WriteLine("<rd:ReportUnitType>Inch</rd:ReportUnitType>");
txtstream.WriteLine("</Report>");
txtstream.Close();
          }
        }
      }
```

The code above not only produces all three files, it also create a DataGridView view of the information you want to display.

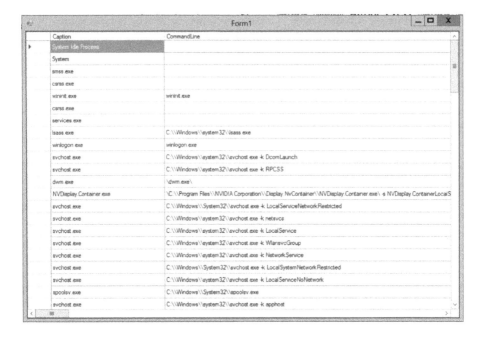

Because all three files are created in harmony with each other, you can change the root\\cimv2 to any other namespace and the class to any other class you want to use that is supported by the namespace. Just remember to change the Products in the filename to another name. I generally cut off the part of the name just past the first underscore. Which I did with the example. Instead of Win32_Products, I used Products. But you can do it any way you want.

CREATING THE REPORT APPLICATION FORM

Below is the form code:

```
using System;
using System.Collections.Generic;
using System.ComponentModel;
using System.Data;
using System.Drawing;
using System.Linq;
using System.Text;
using System.Threading.Tasks;
using System.Windows.Forms;

namespace WindowsFormsApp12
{
```

The InitializeComponent().void file:

```csharp
namespace WindowsFormsApp12
{
    partial class Form1
    {
        /// <summary>
        /// Required designer variable.
        /// </summary>
        private System.ComponentModel.IContainer components =
null;

        /// <summary>
        /// Clean up any resources being used.
        /// </summary>
        /// <param name="disposing">true if managed resources
should be disposed; otherwise, false.</param>
        protected override void Dispose(bool disposing)
        {
            if (disposing && (components != null))
            {
                components.Dispose();
            }
            base.Dispose(disposing);
        }

        #region Windows Form Designer generated code

        /// <summary>
        /// Required method for Designer support - do not modify
        /// the contents of this method with the code editor.
        /// </summary>
        private void InitializeComponent()
        {
            this.reportViewer1 = new
Microsoft.Reporting.WinForms.ReportViewer();
            this.SuspendLayout();
            //
            // reportViewer1
            //
            this.reportViewer1.Dock =
System.Windows.Forms.DockStyle.Fill;
            this.reportViewer1.Location = new
System.Drawing.Point(0, 0);
```

```
                this.reportViewer1.Name = "ReportViewer";
                this.reportViewer1.Size = new
System.Drawing.Size(800, 450);
                this.reportViewer1.TabIndex = 0;
                //
                // Form1
                //
                this.AutoScaleDimensions = new
System.Drawing.SizeF(8F, 16F);
                this.AutoScaleMode =
System.Windows.Forms.AutoScaleMode.Font;
                this.ClientSize = new System.Drawing.Size(800, 450);
                this.Controls.Add(this.reportViewer1);
                this.Name = "Form1";
                this.Text = "Form1";
                this.Load += new
System.EventHandler(this.Form1_Load);
                this.ResumeLayout(false);

        }

        #endregion

        private Microsoft.Reporting.WinForms.ReportViewer
reportViewer1;
    }
}
```

Code for the Form Load:

```
    System.Data.DataSet ds = new System.Data.DataSet();

ds.ReadXml("C:\\Users\\Administrator\\source\\repos\\WindowsFormsApp18\\WindowsFormsApp18\\EventLog.xml");

        reportViewer1.LocalReport.ReportPath =
"C:\\Users\\Administrator\\source\\repos\\WindowsFormsApp18\\WindowsFormsApp18\\EventLog.rdlc";
        reportViewer1.LocalReport.DataSources.Clear();
        reportViewer1.LocalReport.DataSources.Add(new
Microsoft.Reporting.WinForms.ReportDataSource("DataSet1", ds.Tables[0]));
        this.reportViewer1.RefreshReport();
```

And the output:

Form1

Archive	Caption	CreationDate	CSName	Description	Drive	FileName
TRUE	c:\\windows\\system32\\winevt\\logs\\application.evtx	02/05/202019:08:46	WIN-VRKHLADIDGT	c:\\windows\\system32\\winevt\\logs\\application.evtx	c:	Application
TRUE	c:\\windows\\system32\\winevt\\logs\\oalerts.evtx	02/06/202006:16:26	WIN-VRKHLADIDGT	c:\\windows\\system32\\winevt\\logs\\oalerts.evtx	c:	OAlerts
TRUE	c:\\windows\\system32\\winevt\\logs\\osession.evtx	02/05/202021:21:11	WIN-VRKHLADIDGT	c:\\windows\\system32\\winevt\\logs\\osession.evtx	c:	OSession
TRUE	c:\\windows\\system32\\winevt\\logs\\security.evtx	02/05/202019:08:46	WIN-VRKHLADIDGT	c:\\windows\\system32\\winevt\\logs\\security.evtx	c:	Security
TRUE	c:\\windows\\system32\\winevt\\logs\\system.evtx	02/05/202019:08:46	WIN-VRKHLADIDGT	c:\\windows\\system32\\winevt\\logs\\system.evtx	c:	System
TRUE	c:\\windows\\system32\\winevt\\logs\\windows powershell.evtx	02/05/202019:08:46	WIN-VRKHLADIDGT	c:\\windows\\system32\\winevt\\logs\\windows.powershell.evtx	c:	Windows f

CREATING REPORTS USING THE FILE SYSTEM OBJECT

Create A Report on all executables in the C:\Windows\System32 directory

This one is also pretty straight forward. It is just time consuming. We're going to enumerate through all the folders, look for the exe extension and display it in a report. It will include the name of the file, its full path, Date Created, Date Last Modified and Date Last Accessed.

Well, this took less time than I thought it would. Plus, the code is simple and to the point. Before we go into the code, one entry made me laugh:

Someone seems to enjoy watching InspectorGadget.

Back to work. You need to create new C#.Net Windows Form Application and include the

Okay, so here's the code:

```csharp
using System;
using System.Collections.Generic;
using System.ComponentModel;
using System.Data;
using System.Drawing;
using System.Linq;
using System.Text;
using System.Threading.Tasks;
using System.Windows.Forms;
using Scripting;
namespace WindowsFormsApp13
{
    public partial class Form1 : Form
    {
        public Form1()
        {
            InitializeComponent();
        }

        System.Data.DataSet ds = new System.Data.DataSet();
        System.Data.DataTable dt = new System.Data.DataTable();
        private void Form1_Load(object sender, EventArgs e)
        {

            dt.Columns.Add("Filename");
            dt.Columns.Add("Path");
            dt.Columns.Add("DateCreated");
            dt.Columns.Add("DateLastModified");
            dt.Columns.Add("DateLastAccessed");


            int[] b = new int[5];
            string[] Names = new string[5];

            Names[0] = "Filename";
            Names[1] = "Path";
            Names[2] = "DateCreated";
            Names[3] = "DateLastModified";
            Names[4] = "DateLastAccessed";

            FileSystemObject fso = new FileSystemObject();
            Folder fldr = fso.GetFolder("C:\\Windows\\System32");
```

```csharp
        EnumFolders(fldr);

        ds.Tables.Add(dt);
        ds.WriteXml(Application.StartupPath + "\\executables.xml");
        ds.WriteXmlSchema(Application.StartupPath + "\\executables.xsd");

        dataGridView1.DataSource = ds.Tables[0];

        for (int a = 0; a < dataGridView1.Columns.Count; a++)
        {
            b[a] = dataGridView1.Rows[0].Cells[a].Size.Width / 70;
        }

        create_Report(Names, b);

    }
    public void EnumFolders(Folder folder)
    {
        if (folder.Files.Count > 0)
        {
            foreach (File f in folder.Files)
            {
                int pos = f.Name.ToLower().IndexOf(".exe");
                if (pos > 0)
                {
                    if (pos + 4 == f.Name.ToString().Length)
                    {
                        System.Data.DataRow dr = dt.NewRow();
                        dr["FileName"] = f.Name;
                        dr["Path"] = f.Path;
                        dr["DateCreated"] = f.DateCreated;
                        dr["DateLastModified"] = f.DateLastModified;
                        dr["DateLastAccessed"] = f.DateLastAccessed;
                        dt.Rows.Add(dr);
                        dt.AcceptChanges();
                    }
                }
            }

        }
        foreach (Folder fldr in folder.SubFolders)
        {
            try
            {
                EnumFolders(fldr);
            }
            catch (Exception ex)
            {

            }
        }
    }
    private void create_Report(String[] Names, int[] L)
    {
        FileSystemObject fso = new FileSystemObject();
        TextStream txtstream = fso.OpenTextFile(Application.StartupPath +
"\\WindowsSystem32Exes.rdlc", IOMode.ForWriting, true, Tristate.TristateUseDefault);
```

```
txtstream.WriteLine("<?xml version=\"1.0\"?>");
txtstream.WriteLine("<Report
xmlns:rd=\"http://schemas.microsoft.com/SQLServer/reporting/reportdesigner\"
xmlns=\"http://schemas.microsoft.com/sqlserver/reporting/2008/01/reportdefinition\">");

txtstream.WriteLine(" <DataSources>");
txtstream.WriteLine("  <DataSource Name=\"WindowsApplication5\">");
txtstream.WriteLine("   <ConnectionProperties>");
txtstream.WriteLine("    <DataProvider>System.Data.DataSet</DataProvider>");
txtstream.WriteLine("    <ConnectString>/* Local Connection */</ConnectString>");
txtstream.WriteLine("   </ConnectionProperties>");
txtstream.WriteLine("   <rd:DataSourceID>4ada475a-519d-4774-8a8e-
cd804357bc15</rd:DataSourceID>");
txtstream.WriteLine("  </DataSource>");
txtstream.WriteLine(" </DataSources>");
txtstream.WriteLine(" <DataSets>");
txtstream.WriteLine("  <DataSet Name=\"DataSet1\">");
txtstream.WriteLine("   <Fields>");

for (int x = 0; x < Names.GetLength(0); x++)
{

    txtstream.WriteLine("    <Field Name=\"" + Names[x] + "\">");

    txtstream.WriteLine("     <DataField>" + Names[x] + "</DataField>");
    txtstream.WriteLine("     <rd:TypeName>System.String</rd:TypeName>");
    txtstream.WriteLine("    </Field>");

}

txtstream.WriteLine("   </Fields>");
txtstream.WriteLine("   <Query>");
txtstream.WriteLine("
<DataSourceName>WindowsApplication5</DataSourceName>");
txtstream.WriteLine("    <CommandText>/* Local Query */</CommandText>");
txtstream.WriteLine("   </Query>");
txtstream.WriteLine("   <rd:DataSetInfo>");
txtstream.WriteLine("
<rd:DataSetName>WindowsApplication5</rd:DataSetName>");
txtstream.WriteLine("    <rd:TableName>data</rd:TableName>");
txtstream.WriteLine("
<rd:ObjectDataSourceSelectMethod>win32_bios</rd:ObjectDataSourceSelectMethod>");
txtstream.WriteLine("    <rd:ObjectDataSourceType>WindowsApplication5.data,
win32_bios.Designer.vb, Version=0.0.0.0, Culture=neutral,
PublicKeyToken=null</rd:ObjectDataSourceType>");
txtstream.WriteLine("   </rd:DataSetInfo>");
txtstream.WriteLine("  </DataSet>");
txtstream.WriteLine(" </DataSets>");
txtstream.WriteLine(" <Body>");
txtstream.WriteLine("  <ReportItems>");
txtstream.WriteLine("   <Tablix Name=\"Tablix1\">");
txtstream.WriteLine("    <TablixBody>");
txtstream.WriteLine("     <TablixColumns>");

for (int x = 0; x < Names.GetLength(0); x++)
{
```

```
    txtstream.WriteLine("          <TablixColumn>");
    txtstream.WriteLine("            <Width>" + L[x] + "in</Width>");
    txtstream.WriteLine("          </TablixColumn>");
}

txtstream.WriteLine("        </TablixColumns>");
txtstream.WriteLine("        <TablixRows>");
txtstream.WriteLine("         <TablixRow>");
txtstream.WriteLine("          <Height>0.25in</Height>");
txtstream.WriteLine("          <TablixCells>");

for (int x = 0; x < Names.GetLength(0); x++)
{

    txtstream.WriteLine("              <TablixCell>");
    txtstream.WriteLine("               <CellContents>");
    txtstream.WriteLine("                <Textbox Name=\"Textbox" + x + 1 + "\">");

    txtstream.WriteLine("                 <CanGrow>true</CanGrow>");
    txtstream.WriteLine("                 <KeepTogether>true</KeepTogether>");
    txtstream.WriteLine("                 <Paragraphs>");
    txtstream.WriteLine("                  <Paragraph>");
    txtstream.WriteLine("                   <TextRuns>");
    txtstream.WriteLine("                    <TextRun>");
    txtstream.WriteLine("                     <Value>" + Names[x] + "</Value>");
    txtstream.WriteLine("                     <Style>");
    txtstream.WriteLine("                      <FontFamily>Tahoma</FontFamily>");
    txtstream.WriteLine("                      <FontSize>11pt</FontSize>");
    txtstream.WriteLine("                      <FontWeight>Bold</FontWeight>");
    txtstream.WriteLine("                      <Color>White</Color>");
    txtstream.WriteLine("                     </Style>");
    txtstream.WriteLine("                    </TextRun>");
    txtstream.WriteLine("                   </TextRuns>");
    txtstream.WriteLine("                   <Style />");
    txtstream.WriteLine("                  </Paragraph>");
    txtstream.WriteLine("                 </Paragraphs>");
    txtstream.WriteLine("                 <rd:DefaultName>Textbox" + x + 1 +
"</rd:DefaultName>");
    txtstream.WriteLine("                 <Style>");
    txtstream.WriteLine("                  <Border>");
    txtstream.WriteLine("                   <Color>#7292cc</Color>");
    txtstream.WriteLine("                   <Style>Solid</Style>");
    txtstream.WriteLine("                  </Border>");
    txtstream.WriteLine("
<BackgroundColor>#4c68a2</BackgroundColor>");
    txtstream.WriteLine("                      <PaddingLeft>2pt</PaddingLeft>");
    txtstream.WriteLine("                      <PaddingRight>2pt</PaddingRight>");
    txtstream.WriteLine("                      <PaddingTop>2pt</PaddingTop>");
    txtstream.WriteLine("                      <PaddingBottom>2pt</PaddingBottom>");
    txtstream.WriteLine("                  </Style>");
    txtstream.WriteLine("                 </Textbox>");
    txtstream.WriteLine("               </CellContents>");
    txtstream.WriteLine("              </TablixCell>");

}
txtstream.WriteLine("          </TablixCells>");
txtstream.WriteLine("         </TablixRow>");
```

```csharp
                txtstream.WriteLine("          <TablixRow>");
                txtstream.WriteLine("            <Height>0.25in</Height>");
                txtstream.WriteLine("            <TablixCells>");

                for (int x = 0; x < Names.GetLength(0); x++)
                {
                    txtstream.WriteLine("              <TablixCell>");
                    txtstream.WriteLine("                <CellContents>");
                    txtstream.WriteLine("                  <Textbox Name=\"" + Names[x] + "\">");

                    txtstream.WriteLine("                    <CanGrow>true</CanGrow>");
                    txtstream.WriteLine("                    <KeepTogether>true</KeepTogether>");
                    txtstream.WriteLine("                    <Paragraphs>");
                    txtstream.WriteLine("                      <Paragraph>");
                    txtstream.WriteLine("                        <TextRuns>");
                    txtstream.WriteLine("                          <TextRun>");
                    txtstream.WriteLine("                            <Value>=Fields!" + Names[x] +
".Value</Value>");
                    txtstream.WriteLine("                            <Style>");
                    txtstream.WriteLine("                              <FontFamily>Tahoma</FontFamily>");
                    txtstream.WriteLine("                              <Color>#4d4d4d</Color>");
                    txtstream.WriteLine("                            </Style>");
                    txtstream.WriteLine("                          </TextRun>");
                    txtstream.WriteLine("                        </TextRuns>");
                    txtstream.WriteLine("                        <Style />");
                    txtstream.WriteLine("                      </Paragraph>");
                    txtstream.WriteLine("                    </Paragraphs>");
                    txtstream.WriteLine("                    <rd:DefaultName>" + Names[x] +
"</rd:DefaultName>");
                    txtstream.WriteLine("                    <Style>");
                    txtstream.WriteLine("                      <Border>");
                    txtstream.WriteLine("                        <Color>#e5e5e5</Color>");
                    txtstream.WriteLine("                        <Style>Solid</Style>");
                    txtstream.WriteLine("                      </Border>");
                    txtstream.WriteLine("                      <PaddingLeft>2pt</PaddingLeft>");
                    txtstream.WriteLine("                      <PaddingRight>2pt</PaddingRight>");
                    txtstream.WriteLine("                      <PaddingTop>2pt</PaddingTop>");
                    txtstream.WriteLine("                      <PaddingBottom>2pt</PaddingBottom>");
                    txtstream.WriteLine("                    </Style>");
                    txtstream.WriteLine("                  </Textbox>");
                    txtstream.WriteLine("                </CellContents>");
                    txtstream.WriteLine("              </TablixCell>");
                }
                txtstream.WriteLine("            </TablixCells>");
                txtstream.WriteLine("          </TablixRow>");
                txtstream.WriteLine("        </TablixRows>");
                txtstream.WriteLine("      </TablixBody>");
                txtstream.WriteLine("      <TablixColumnHierarchy>");
                txtstream.WriteLine("        <TablixMembers>");

                for (int x = 0; x < Names.GetLength(0); x++)
                {

                    txtstream.WriteLine("          <TablixMember />");

                }
```

```
txtstream.WriteLine("        </TablixMembers>");
txtstream.WriteLine("       </TablixColumnHierarchy>");
txtstream.WriteLine("       <TablixRowHierarchy>");
txtstream.WriteLine("        <TablixMembers>");
txtstream.WriteLine("         <TablixMember>");
txtstream.WriteLine("           <KeepWithGroup>After</KeepWithGroup>");
txtstream.WriteLine("         </TablixMember>");
txtstream.WriteLine("         <TablixMember>");
txtstream.WriteLine("           <Group Name=\"Details\"/>");
txtstream.WriteLine("         </TablixMember>");
txtstream.WriteLine("        </TablixMembers>");
txtstream.WriteLine("       </TablixRowHierarchy>");
txtstream.WriteLine("       <DataSetName>DataSet1</DataSetName>");
txtstream.WriteLine("       <Height>0.5in</Height>");
txtstream.WriteLine("       <Width>409.52083in</Width>");
txtstream.WriteLine("       <Style>");
txtstream.WriteLine("        <Border>");
txtstream.WriteLine("          <Style>None</Style>");
txtstream.WriteLine("        </Border>");
txtstream.WriteLine("       </Style>");
txtstream.WriteLine("      </Tablix>");
txtstream.WriteLine("    </ReportItems>");
txtstream.WriteLine("    <Height>2in</Height>");
txtstream.WriteLine("    <Style />");
txtstream.WriteLine("  </Body>");
txtstream.WriteLine("  <Width>409.52083in</Width>");
txtstream.WriteLine("  <Page>");
txtstream.WriteLine("    <LeftMargin>1in</LeftMargin>");
txtstream.WriteLine("    <RightMargin>1in</RightMargin>");
txtstream.WriteLine("    <TopMargin>1in</TopMargin>");
txtstream.WriteLine("    <BottomMargin>1in</BottomMargin>");
txtstream.WriteLine("    <Style />");
txtstream.WriteLine("  </Page>");
txtstream.WriteLine("  <rd:ReportID>7fa7ad8c-6890-4152-8fce-
3e6f01fffd8c</rd:ReportID>");
txtstream.WriteLine("  <rd:ReportUnitType>Inch</rd:ReportUnitType>");
txtstream.WriteLine("</Report>");
txtstream.Close();
        }
    }
}
```

The application also creates a dataGridView:

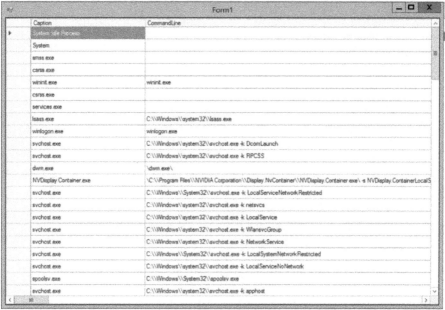

You need to make a reference to the Microsoft.ReportViewer.Windows first after you create the new Application for your reports. Once added, it will show up in your references.

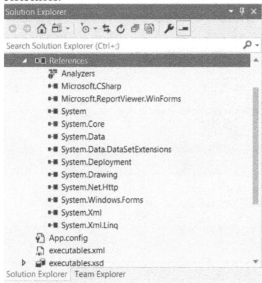

After you have done that, you can add the ReportViewer with the code below to the InitializeComponent: void() file:

```csharp
namespace WindowsFormsApp14
{
    partial class Form1
    {
        /// <summary>
        /// Required designer variable.
        /// </summary>
        private System.ComponentModel.IContainer components = null;

        /// <summary>
        /// Clean up any resources being used.
        /// </summary>
        /// <param name="disposing">true if managed resources should be disposed; otherwise,
        false.</param>
        protected override void Dispose(bool disposing)
        {
            if (disposing && (components != null))
            {
                components.Dispose();
            }
            base.Dispose(disposing);
        }

        #region Windows Form Designer generated code

        /// <summary>
        /// Required method for Designer support - do not modify
        /// the contents of this method with the code editor.
        /// </summary>
        private void InitializeComponent()
        {
            this.reportViewer1 = new Microsoft.Reporting.WinForms.ReportViewer();
            this.SuspendLayout();
            //
            // reportViewer1
            //
            this.reportViewer1.Dock = System.Windows.Forms.DockStyle.Fill;
            this.reportViewer1.Location = new System.Drawing.Point(0, 0);
            this.reportViewer1.Name = "ReportViewer";
            this.reportViewer1.Size = new System.Drawing.Size(800, 450);
            this.reportViewer1.TabIndex = 0;
            //
            // Form1
            //
            this.AutoScaleDimensions = new System.Drawing.SizeF(8F, 16F);
            this.AutoScaleMode = System.Windows.Forms.AutoScaleMode.Font;
            this.ClientSize = new System.Drawing.Size(800, 450);
            this.Controls.Add(this.reportViewer1);
            this.Name = "Form1";
            this.Text = "Form1";
            this.Load += new System.EventHandler(this.Form1_Load);
            this.ResumeLayout(false);

        }
```

```
#endregion
      private Microsoft.Reporting.WinForms.ReportViewer reportViewer1;
  }
}
```

After that, it is just a matter of adding the code to the form1_Load() event:

```csharp
using System;
using System.Collections.Generic;
using System.ComponentModel;
using System.Data;
using System.Drawing;
using System.Linq;
using System.Text;
using System.Threading.Tasks;
using System.Windows.Forms;

namespace WindowsFormsApp14
{
    public partial class Form1 : Form
    {
        public Form1()
        {
            InitializeComponent();
        }

        private void Form1_Load(object sender, EventArgs e)
        {
            System.Data.DataSet ds = new System.Data.DataSet();

ds.ReadXml("C:\\Users\\Administrator\\source\\repos\\WindowsFormsApp14\\WindowsFormsApp14\\executables.xml");

            reportViewer1.LocalReport.ReportPath =
"C:\\Users\\Administrator\\source\\repos\\WindowsFormsApp14\\WindowsFormsApp14\\WindowsSystem32Exes.rdlc";
            reportViewer1.LocalReport.DataSources.Clear();
            reportViewer1.LocalReport.DataSources.Add(new
Microsoft.Reporting.WinForms.ReportDataSource("DataSet1", ds.Tables[0]));
            this.reportViewer1.RefreshReport();

        }
    }
}
```

When you run your own version of this program, you should see this:

14 4 1   of 27 ▶ ▶| ⊕ ⊗ ☁ 🔍   🖨 🗋 🗐 🖫 ▾   [75%] ▾   Find | Next

Filename	Path	DateCreated	DateLastModified	DateLastAccessed
appverf.exe	C:\Windows\System32\appverif.exe	3/18/2019 6:45:38 PM	3/18/2019 6:46:38 PM	2/14/2020 7:13:58 AM
ARP.EXE	C:\Windows\System32\ARP.EXE	3/14/2020 12:58:58 PM	1/19/2016 9:39:01 AM	3/14/2020 12:58:53 PM
at.exe	C:\Windows\System32\at.exe	2/18/2020 1:18:40 AM	10/28/2014 6:51:50 PM	2/18/2020 1:58:40 AM
AtBroker.exe	C:\Windows\System32\AtBroker.exe	3/18/2020 1:18:40 AM	10/28/2014 6:43:28 PM	3/18/2020 1:18:40 AM
attrib.exe	C:\Windows\System32\attrib.exe	3/18/2020 1:19:34 AM	10/28/2014 6:05:13 PM	3/18/2020 1:19:24 AM
auditpol.exe	C:\Windows\System32\auditpol.exe	3/18/2020 1:19:38 AM	10/28/2014 6:04:58 PM	3/18/2020 1:19:38 AM
autochk.exe	C:\Windows\System32\autochk.exe	2/14/2020 6:42:08 AM	2/22/2014 4:24:36 AM	2/14/2020 6:42:08 AM
autoconv.exe	C:\Windows\System32\autoconv.exe	3/14/2020 7:31:02 AM	8/6/2017 11:03:31 PM	3/16/2020 7:31:02 AM
autofmt.exe	C:\Windows\System32\autofmt.exe	2/14/2020 6:42:08 AM	2/22/2014 4:24:35 AM	2/14/2020 6:42:08 AM
BackgroundTaskHost.exe	C:\Windows\System32\BackgroundTaskHost.exe	1/18/2020 1:18:42 AM	10/28/2014 6:05:28 PM	1/18/2020 1:18:42 AM
BackgroundTransferHost.exe	C:\Windows\System32\BackgroundTransferHost.exe	3/16/2020 1:19:11 AM	10/26/2014 6:00:12 PM	3/18/2020 1:19:11 AM
bitsadmin.exe	C:\Windows\System32\bitsadmin.exe	3/18/2020 1:18:42 AM	10/28/2014 6:39:42 PM	3/18/2020 1:18:42 AM
bootcfg.exe	C:\Windows\System32\bootcfg.exe	3/18/2020 1:18:43 AM	10/28/2014 6:47:08 PM	3/18/2020 1:18:43 AM
ByteCodeGenerator.exe	C:\Windows\System32\ByteCodeGenerator.exe	3/18/2020 1:17:37 AM	10/28/2014 5:46:17 PM	3/18/2020 1:17:37 AM
cacls.exe	C:\Windows\System32\cacls.exe	3/18/2020 1:18:39 AM	10/28/2014 6:04:52 PM	3/18/2020 1:18:39 AM
calc.exe	C:\Windows\System32\calc.exe	3/14/2020 12:57:01 PM	1/31/2016 6:51:09 PM	3/14/2020 12:57:01 PM
CameraSettingsUIHost.exe	C:\Windows\System32\CameraSettingsUIHost.exe	3/18/2020 1:20:19 AM	10/26/2014 6:11:11 PM	3/18/2020 1:20:19 AM
CertEnrollCtrl.exe	C:\Windows\System32\CertEnrollCtrl.exe	3/15/2020 10:43:16 AM	10/28/2014 5:50:25 PM	3/15/2020 10:43:16 AM
certreq.exe	C:\Windows\System32\certreq.exe	3/18/2020 1:18:45 AM	10/28/2014 6:26:40 PM	3/18/2020 1:18:45 AM
certutil.exe	C:\Windows\System32\certutil.exe	3/16/2020 7:31:11 AM	3/8/2018 9:59:09 AM	3/16/2020 7:31:11 AM
change.exe	C:\Windows\System32\change.exe	3/18/2020 1:18:16 AM	10/28/2014 6:56:38 PM	3/18/2020 1:18:16 AM
charmap.exe	C:\Windows\System32\charmap.exe	3/18/2020 1:17:38 AM	10/28/2014 6:47:41 PM	3/18/2020 1:17:38 AM
CheckNetIsolation.exe	C:\Windows\System32\CheckNetIsolation.exe	3/18/2020 1:20:26 AM	10/28/2014 5:44:34 PM	3/18/2020 1:20:26 AM
chglogon.exe	C:\Windows\System32\chglogon.exe	3/18/2020 1:18:16 AM	10/28/2014 6:56:34 PM	3/18/2020 1:18:16 AM
chgport.exe	C:\Windows\System32\chgport.exe	3/18/2020 1:18:16 AM	10/28/2014 6:58:00 PM	3/18/2020 1:18:16 AM
chgusr.exe	C:\Windows\System32\chgusr.exe	3/18/2020 1:18:16 AM	10/28/2014 6:58:28 PM	3/18/2020 1:18:16 AM
chkdsk.exe	C:\Windows\System32\chkdsk.exe	3/18/2020 1:18:45 AM	10/28/2014 6:03:12 PM	3/18/2020 1:18:45 AM
chkntfs.exe	C:\Windows\System32\chkntfs.exe	3/18/2020 1:18:42 AM	10/28/2014 6:58:25 PM	3/16/2020 1:18:42 AM
choice.exe	C:\Windows\System32\choice.exe	3/18/2020 1:18:45 AM	10/28/2014 6:46:32 PM	3/18/2020 1:18:45 AM
cipher.exe	C:\Windows\System32\cipher.exe	3/18/2020 1:18:45 AM	10/28/2014 6:45:36 PM	3/18/2020 1:18:45 AM
cleanmgr.exe	C:\Windows\System32\cleanmgr.exe	3/18/2020 1:17:39 AM	10/28/2014 6:38:02 PM	3/18/2020 1:17:39 AM
clconfg.exe	C:\Windows\System32\clconfg.exe	3/18/2020 1:19:11 AM	3/26/2014 6:58:20 PM	3/18/2020 1:19:11 AM
clip.exe	C:\Windows\System32\clip.exe	3/18/2020 1:18:45 AM	10/28/2014 6:51:29 PM	3/18/2020 1:18:45 AM
cmd.exe	C:\Windows\System32\cmd.exe	3/18/2020 1:17:39 AM	10/28/2014 6:05:26 PM	3/18/2020 1:17:39 AM
cmdkey.exe	C:\Windows\System32\cmdkey.exe	3/18/2020 1:19:57 AM	10/28/2014 6:58:13 PM	3/18/2020 1:19:57 AM
cmd32.exe	C:\Windows\System32\cmd32.exe	3/18/2020 1:18:08 AM	10/28/2014 6:48:18 PM	3/18/2020 1:18:08 AM
cmmon32.exe	C:\Windows\System32\cmmon32.exe	3/18/2020 1:18:09 AM	10/28/2014 6:58:13 PM	3/18/2020 1:18:09 AM
cmstp.exe	C:\Windows\System32\cmstp.exe	3/18/2020 1:18:29 AM	10/28/2014 6:33:17 PM	3/18/2020 1:18:29 AM
colorcpl.exe	C:\Windows\System32\colorcpl.exe	3/18/2020 1:17:46 AM	10/28/2014 6:58:19 PM	3/18/2020 1:17:46 AM

While simple, it is also time consuming. For example, if you decided to run this against your windows drive: C:\ , it could take a good hour or longer. But, at least, you know you can do this through code.

CREATING REPORTS USING THE POWER OF WMI

Go from 0 to done in less than 5 minutes

That is, once you've created the entire template listed below, first.

As you might remember, I told you that it took 12 minutes to create the xml, xsd and then create a report from the xml and xsd.

Why not do all of it through automation?

Well, it can be done.

But I tried doing it and realized it would take longer than what it was worth. For example, when I copied the files from one location to another, all of the files were point to the original directory and when you make any changes, all of the references to all the rest of the files also needs to be changed.

With that said, you can create a generic application and add a generic xsd, xml and rdlc file as shown below and then populate it, through automation and run the report in less than 5 minutes.

Which is close to 1/3rd the time.

All you have to do is create a generic application, add the blank xsd, xml and report forms, put the Report Viewer control on the form. Then fill each with the information needed to make it work.

```
using System;
using System.Collections.Generic;
using System.ComponentModel;
using System.Data;
using System.Drawing;
using System.Linq;
using System.Text;
```

```csharp
using System.Threading.Tasks;
using System.Windows.Forms;
using WbemScripting;
using Scripting;

namespace WindowsFormsApp11
{
    public partial class Form1 : Form
    {
        public Form1()
        {
            InitializeComponent();
        }
        private string GetValue(string n, SWbemObject obj)
        {
            int pos = 0;
            string tn = n;
            string tempstr = obj.GetObjectText_();
            tn += " =";
            pos = tempstr.IndexOf(tn);
            if (pos > 0)
            {
                pos = pos + tn.Length;
                tempstr = tempstr.Substring(pos, tempstr.Length - pos);
                pos = tempstr.IndexOf(";");
                tempstr = tempstr.Substring(0, pos);
                tempstr = tempstr.Replace("{", "");
                tempstr = tempstr.Replace("}", "");
                tempstr = tempstr.Replace("\"", "");
                tempstr = tempstr.Trim();
                if (obj.Properties_.Item(n).CIMType ==
WbemScripting.WbemCimtypeEnum.wbemCimtypeDatetime && tempstr.Length > 14)
                {
                    return ReturnDateTime(tempstr);
                }
                else
                {
                    return tempstr;
                }
            }
            else
            {
                return "";
            }
        }
        private string ReturnDateTime(string Value)
```

```csharp
        {
            return Value.Substring(4, 2) + "/" + Value.Substring(6, 2) + "/" + Value.Substring(0,
4) + "" + Value.Substring(8, 2) + ":" + Value.Substring(10, 2) + ":" + Value.Substring(12, 2);
        }

        private void Form1_Load(object sender, EventArgs e)
        {
            int[] b = null;
            string[] Names = null;
            DataSet ds = new DataSet();
            DataTable dt = new DataTable();
            ds.Tables.Add(dt);
            WbemScripting.SWbemLocator l = new WbemScripting.SWbemLocator();
            WbemScripting.SWbemServices svc = l.ConnectServer(".", "root\\cimv2");
            svc.Security_.AuthenticationLevel =
WbemAuthenticationLevelEnum.wbemAuthenticationLevelPktPrivacy;
            svc.Security_.ImpersonationLevel =
WbemImpersonationLevelEnum.wbemImpersonationLevelImpersonate;
            SWbemObjectSet objs = svc.InstancesOf("Win32_Process");
            int x = 0;
            foreach (SWbemObject obj in objs)
            {
                b = new int[obj.Properties_.Count];
                Names = new string[obj.Properties_.Count];
                foreach(SWbemProperty prop in obj.Properties_)
                {
                    ds.Tables[0].Columns.Add(prop.Name);
                    dataGridView1.Columns.Add(prop.Name, prop.Name);
                    Names[x] = prop.Name;
                    x = x + 1;

                }
                break;
            }
            x = 0;
            int y = 0;
            foreach (SWbemObject obj in objs)
            {
                dataGridView1.Rows.Add();
                DataRow dr = ds.Tables[0].NewRow();
                foreach (SWbemProperty prop in obj.Properties_)
                {
                    dr[x] = GetValue(prop.Name, obj);
                    dataGridView1.Rows[y].Cells[x].Value = GetValue(prop.Name, obj);
                    x = x + 1;
                }
```

```csharp
            ds.Tables[0].Rows.Add(dr);
            x = 0;
            y = y + 1;
        }
        ds.Tables[0].AcceptChanges();

        for (int a = 0; a < dataGridView1.Columns.Count; a++)
        {
            b[a] = dataGridView1.Rows[0].Cells[a].Size.Width/70;
        }
        ds.WriteXml(Application.StartupPath + "\\Process.xml");
        ds.WriteXmlSchema(Application.StartupPath + "\\Process.xsd");
        create_Report(Names, b);
    }
    private void create_Report(String[]Names, int[] L)
    {
        FileSystemObject fso = new FileSystemObject();
        TextStream txtstream = fso.OpenTextFile(Application.StartupPath + "\\Process.rdlc",
IOMode.ForWriting, true, Tristate.TristateUseDefault);
        txtstream.WriteLine("<?xml version=\"1.0\"?>");
        txtstream.WriteLine("<Report
xmlns:rd=\"http://schemas.microsoft.com/SQLServer/reporting/reportdesigner\"
xmlns=\"http://schemas.microsoft.com/sqlserver/reporting/2008/01/reportdefinition\">");

        txtstream.WriteLine(" <DataSources>");
        txtstream.WriteLine("  <DataSource Name=\"WindowsApplication5\">");
        txtstream.WriteLine("   <ConnectionProperties>");
        txtstream.WriteLine("    <DataProvider>System.Data.DataSet</DataProvider>");
        txtstream.WriteLine("    <ConnectString>/* Local Connection
*/</ConnectString>");
        txtstream.WriteLine("   </ConnectionProperties>");
        txtstream.WriteLine("   <rd:DataSourceID>4ada475a-519d-4774-8a8e-
cd804357bc15</rd:DataSourceID>");
        txtstream.WriteLine("  </DataSource>");
        txtstream.WriteLine(" </DataSources>");
        txtstream.WriteLine(" <DataSets>");
        txtstream.WriteLine("  <DataSet Name=\"DataSet1\">");
        txtstream.WriteLine("   <Fields>");

        for (int x = 0; x < Names.GetLength(0); x++)
        {

            txtstream.WriteLine("    <Field Name=\"" + Names[x] + "\">");

            txtstream.WriteLine("     <DataField>" + Names[x] + "</DataField>");
            txtstream.WriteLine("     <rd:TypeName>System.String</rd:TypeName>");
```

```
                    txtstream.WriteLine("      </Field>");

            }

            txtstream.WriteLine("     </Fields>");
            txtstream.WriteLine("     <Query>");
            txtstream.WriteLine("
<DataSourceName>WindowsApplication5</DataSourceName>");
            txtstream.WriteLine("       <CommandText>/* Local Query */</CommandText>");
            txtstream.WriteLine("     </Query>");
            txtstream.WriteLine("     <rd:DataSetInfo>");
            txtstream.WriteLine("
<rd:DataSetName>WindowsApplication5</rd:DataSetName>");
            txtstream.WriteLine("       <rd:TableName>data</rd:TableName>");
            txtstream.WriteLine("
<rd:ObjectDataSourceSelectMethod>win32_bios</rd:ObjectDataSourceSelectMethod>");
            txtstream.WriteLine("       <rd:ObjectDataSourceType>WindowsApplication5.data,
win32_bios.Designer.vb, Version=0.0.0.0, Culture=neutral,
PublicKeyToken=null</rd:ObjectDataSourceType>");
            txtstream.WriteLine("     </rd:DataSetInfo>");
            txtstream.WriteLine("    </DataSet>");
            txtstream.WriteLine("  </DataSets>");
            txtstream.WriteLine("  <Body>");
            txtstream.WriteLine("   <ReportItems>");
            txtstream.WriteLine("    <Tablix Name=\"Tablix1\">");
            txtstream.WriteLine("      <TablixBody>");
            txtstream.WriteLine("       <TablixColumns>");

            for (int x = 0; x < Names.GetLength(0); x++)
            {

                txtstream.WriteLine("         <TablixColumn>");
                txtstream.WriteLine("          <Width>" + L[x] + "in</Width>");
                txtstream.WriteLine("         </TablixColumn>");
            }

            txtstream.WriteLine("       </TablixColumns>");
            txtstream.WriteLine("       <TablixRows>");
            txtstream.WriteLine("        <TablixRow>");
            txtstream.WriteLine("         <Height>0.25in</Height>");
            txtstream.WriteLine("         <TablixCells>");

            for (int x = 0; x < Names.GetLength(0); x++)
            {

                txtstream.WriteLine("           <TablixCell>");
```

```
txtstream.WriteLine("                    <CellContents>");
txtstream.WriteLine("                     <Textbox Name=\"Textbox" + x + 1 + "\">");

txtstream.WriteLine("                       <CanGrow>true</CanGrow>");
txtstream.WriteLine("                       <KeepTogether>true</KeepTogether>");
txtstream.WriteLine("                      <Paragraphs>");
txtstream.WriteLine("                       <Paragraph>");
txtstream.WriteLine("                        <TextRuns>");
txtstream.WriteLine("                         <TextRun>");
txtstream.WriteLine("                          <Value>" + Names[x] + "</Value>");
txtstream.WriteLine("                          <Style>");
txtstream.WriteLine("                           <FontFamily>Tahoma</FontFamily>");
txtstream.WriteLine("                           <FontSize>11pt</FontSize>");
txtstream.WriteLine("                           <FontWeight>Bold</FontWeight>");
txtstream.WriteLine("                           <Color>White</Color>");
txtstream.WriteLine("                          </Style>");
txtstream.WriteLine("                         </TextRun>");
txtstream.WriteLine("                        </TextRuns>");
txtstream.WriteLine("                        <Style />");
txtstream.WriteLine("                       </Paragraph>");
txtstream.WriteLine("                      </Paragraphs>");
txtstream.WriteLine("                     <rd:DefaultName>Textbox" + x + 1 +
"</rd:DefaultName>");
txtstream.WriteLine("                     <Style>");
txtstream.WriteLine("                      <Border>");
txtstream.WriteLine("                       <Color>#7292cc</Color>");
txtstream.WriteLine("                       <Style>Solid</Style>");
txtstream.WriteLine("                      </Border>");
txtstream.WriteLine("
<BackgroundColor>#4c68a2</BackgroundColor>");
txtstream.WriteLine("                        <PaddingLeft>2pt</PaddingLeft>");
txtstream.WriteLine("                        <PaddingRight>2pt</PaddingRight>");
txtstream.WriteLine("                        <PaddingTop>2pt</PaddingTop>");
txtstream.WriteLine("                        <PaddingBottom>2pt</PaddingBottom>");
txtstream.WriteLine("                      </Style>");
txtstream.WriteLine("                     </Textbox>");
txtstream.WriteLine("                    </CellContents>");
txtstream.WriteLine("                   </TablixCell>");

}
txtstream.WriteLine("        </TablixCells>");
txtstream.WriteLine("       </TablixRow>");
txtstream.WriteLine("      <TablixRow>");
txtstream.WriteLine("       <Height>0.25in</Height>");
txtstream.WriteLine("        <TablixCells>");
```

```csharp
for (int x = 0; x < Names.GetLength(0); x++)
{
    txtstream.WriteLine("            <TablixCell>");
    txtstream.WriteLine("              <CellContents>");
    txtstream.WriteLine("                <Textbox Name=\"" + Names[x] + "\">");

    txtstream.WriteLine("                  <CanGrow>true</CanGrow>");
    txtstream.WriteLine("                  <KeepTogether>true</KeepTogether>");
    txtstream.WriteLine("                  <Paragraphs>");
    txtstream.WriteLine("                   <Paragraph>");
    txtstream.WriteLine("                    <TextRuns>");
    txtstream.WriteLine("                     <TextRun>");
    txtstream.WriteLine("                      <Value>=Fields!" + Names[x] +
".Value</Value>");
    txtstream.WriteLine("                       <Style>");
    txtstream.WriteLine("                        <FontFamily>Tahoma</FontFamily>");
    txtstream.WriteLine("                        <Color>#4d4d4d</Color>");
    txtstream.WriteLine("                       </Style>");
    txtstream.WriteLine("                     </TextRun>");
    txtstream.WriteLine("                    </TextRuns>");
    txtstream.WriteLine("                    <Style />");
    txtstream.WriteLine("                   </Paragraph>");
    txtstream.WriteLine("                  </Paragraphs>");
    txtstream.WriteLine("                  <rd:DefaultName>" + Names[x] +
"</rd:DefaultName>");
    txtstream.WriteLine("                  <Style>");
    txtstream.WriteLine("                   <Border>");
    txtstream.WriteLine("                    <Color>#e5e5e5</Color>");
    txtstream.WriteLine("                    <Style>Solid</Style>");
    txtstream.WriteLine("                   </Border>");
    txtstream.WriteLine("                   <PaddingLeft>2pt</PaddingLeft>");
    txtstream.WriteLine("                   <PaddingRight>2pt</PaddingRight>");
    txtstream.WriteLine("                   <PaddingTop>2pt</PaddingTop>");
    txtstream.WriteLine("                   <PaddingBottom>2pt</PaddingBottom>");
    txtstream.WriteLine("                  </Style>");
    txtstream.WriteLine("                </Textbox>");
    txtstream.WriteLine("              </CellContents>");
    txtstream.WriteLine("            </TablixCell>");

}

txtstream.WriteLine("          </TablixCells>");
txtstream.WriteLine("         </TablixRow>");
txtstream.WriteLine("        </TablixRows>");
txtstream.WriteLine("      </TablixBody>");
txtstream.WriteLine("      <TablixColumnHierarchy>");
```

```csharp
            txtstream.WriteLine("        <TablixMembers>");

            for (int x = 0; x < Names.GetLength(0); x++)
            {

                txtstream.WriteLine("          <TablixMember />");

            }

            txtstream.WriteLine("        </TablixMembers>");
            txtstream.WriteLine("       </TablixColumnHierarchy>");
            txtstream.WriteLine("       <TablixRowHierarchy>");
            txtstream.WriteLine("        <TablixMembers>");
            txtstream.WriteLine("         <TablixMember>");
            txtstream.WriteLine("          <KeepWithGroup>After</KeepWithGroup>");
            txtstream.WriteLine("         </TablixMember>");
            txtstream.WriteLine("         <TablixMember>");
            txtstream.WriteLine("          <Group Name=\"Details\"/>");
            txtstream.WriteLine("         </TablixMember>");
            txtstream.WriteLine("        </TablixMembers>");
            txtstream.WriteLine("       </TablixRowHierarchy>");
            txtstream.WriteLine("       <DataSetName>DataSet1</DataSetName>");
            txtstream.WriteLine("       <Height>0.5in</Height>");
            txtstream.WriteLine("       <Width>409.52083in</Width>");
            txtstream.WriteLine("       <Style>");
            txtstream.WriteLine("        <Border>");
            txtstream.WriteLine("         <Style>None</Style>");
            txtstream.WriteLine("        </Border>");
            txtstream.WriteLine("       </Style>");
            txtstream.WriteLine("      </Tablix>");
            txtstream.WriteLine("    </ReportItems>");
            txtstream.WriteLine("    <Height>2in</Height>");
            txtstream.WriteLine("    <Style />");
            txtstream.WriteLine("  </Body>");
            txtstream.WriteLine("  <Width>409.52083in</Width>");
            txtstream.WriteLine("  <Page>");
            txtstream.WriteLine("    <LeftMargin>1in</LeftMargin>");
            txtstream.WriteLine("    <RightMargin>1in</RightMargin>");
            txtstream.WriteLine("    <TopMargin>1in</TopMargin>");
            txtstream.WriteLine("    <BottomMargin>1in</BottomMargin>");
            txtstream.WriteLine("    <Style />");
            txtstream.WriteLine("  </Page>");
            txtstream.WriteLine("  <rd:ReportID>7fa7ad8c-6890-4152-8fce-3e6f01fffd8c</rd:ReportID>");
            txtstream.WriteLine("  <rd:ReportUnitType>Inch</rd:ReportUnitType>");
            txtstream.WriteLine("</Report>");
```

```
        txtstream.Close();
    }
  }
}
```

The code above not only produces all three files, it also create a DataGridView
view of the information you want to display in the report:

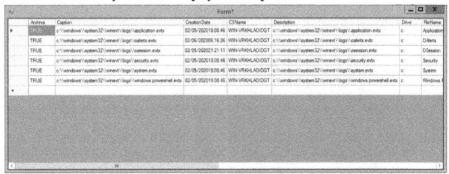

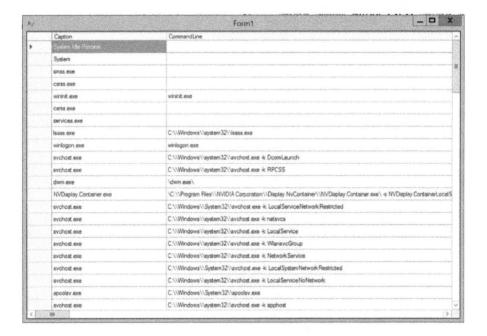

Because all three files are created in harmony with each other, you can change
the root\\cimv2 to any other namespace and the class to any other class you want to
use that is supported by the namespace. Just remember to change the Products in the

filename to another name. I generally cut off the part of the name just past the first underscore. Which I did with the example. Instead of Win32_Products, I used Products. But you can do it any way you want.

CREATING THE REPORT APPLICATION FORM

Below is the form code:

```
using System;
using System.Collections.Generic;
using System.ComponentModel;
using System.Data;
using System.Drawing;
using System.Linq;
using System.Text;
using System.Threading.Tasks;
using System.Windows.Forms;

namespace WindowsFormsApp12
{
    public partial class Form1 : Form
    {
        public Form1()
        {
            InitializeComponent();
        }

        private void Form1_Load(object sender, EventArgs e)
        {
            reportViewer1.LocalReport.ReportPath =
"C:\\Users\\Administrator\\source\\repos\\WindowsFormsApp12\\WindowsFormsApp1
2\\Process.rdlc";
            reportViewer1.LocalReport.DataSources.Clear();
            DataSet ds = new DataSet();

ds.ReadXml("C:\\Users\\Administrator\\source\\repos\\WindowsFormsApp12\\Windo
wsFormsApp12\\Process.xml");
            reportViewer1.LocalReport.DataSources.Add(new
Microsoft.Reporting.WinForms.ReportDataSource("DataSet1", ds.Tables[0]));
            reportViewer1.RefreshReport();
        }
    }
}
```

The InitializeComponent().void file:

```
namespace WindowsFormsApp12
{
    partial class Form1
    {
```

```csharp
        /// <summary>
        /// Required designer variable.
        /// </summary>
        private System.ComponentModel.IContainer components =
null;

        /// <summary>
        /// Clean up any resources being used.
        /// </summary>
        /// <param name="disposing">true if managed resources
should be disposed; otherwise, false.</param>
        protected override void Dispose(bool disposing)
        {
            if (disposing && (components != null))
            {
                components.Dispose();
            }
            base.Dispose(disposing);
        }

        #region Windows Form Designer generated code

        /// <summary>
        /// Required method for Designer support - do not modify
        /// the contents of this method with the code editor.
        /// </summary>
        private void InitializeComponent()
        {
            this.reportViewer1 = new
Microsoft.Reporting.WinForms.ReportViewer();
            this.SuspendLayout();
            //
            // reportViewer1
            //
            this.reportViewer1.Dock =
System.Windows.Forms.DockStyle.Fill;
            this.reportViewer1.Location = new
System.Drawing.Point(0, 0);
            this.reportViewer1.Name = "ReportViewer";
            this.reportViewer1.Size = new
System.Drawing.Size(800, 450);
            this.reportViewer1.TabIndex = 0;
            //
            // Form1
            //
```

```csharp
            this.AutoScaleDimensions = new
System.Drawing.SizeF(8F, 16F);
            this.AutoScaleMode =
System.Windows.Forms.AutoScaleMode.Font;
            this.ClientSize = new System.Drawing.Size(800, 450);
            this.Controls.Add(this.reportViewer1);
            this.Name = "Form1";
            this.Text = "Form1";
            this.Load += new
System.EventHandler(this.Form1_Load);
            this.ResumeLayout(false);

        }

        #endregion

        private Microsoft.Reporting.WinForms.ReportViewer
reportViewer1;
    }
}
```

And the output:

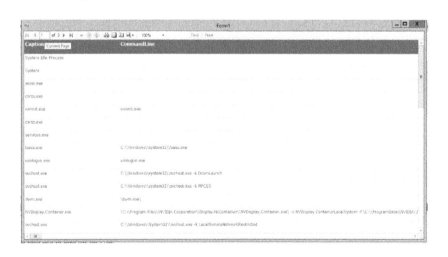

THE FIX PART 2

```
namespace WindowsFormsApp5
{
    partial class Form1
    {
        /// <summary>
        /// Required designer variable.
        /// </summary>
        private System.ComponentModel.IContainer components =
null;

        /// <summary>
        /// Clean up any resources being used.
        /// </summary>
        /// <param name="disposing">true if managed resources
should be disposed; otherwise, false.</param>
        protected override void Dispose(bool disposing)
        {
            if (disposing && (components != null))
            {
                components.Dispose();
            }
            base.Dispose(disposing);
        }
```

```
        #region Windows Form Designer generated code

        /// <summary>
        /// Required method for Designer support - do not modify
        /// the contents of this method with the code editor.
        /// </summary>
        private void InitializeComponent()
        {
            this.components = new
System.ComponentModel.Container();
            this.SuspendLayout();
            //
            // Form1
            //
            this.AutoScaleDimensions = new
System.Drawing.SizeF(8F, 16F);
            this.AutoScaleMode =
System.Windows.Forms.AutoScaleMode.Font;
            this.ClientSize = new System.Drawing.Size(800, 450);
            this.Name = "Form1";
            this.Text = "Form1";
            this.ResumeLayout(false);

        }

        #endregion
    }
}
```

Here's the things we want to add:

```
namespace WindowsFormsApp5
{
    partial class Form1
    {
        /// <summary>
        /// Required designer variable.
        /// </summary>
        private System.ComponentModel.IContainer components =
null;
```

```csharp
        /// <summary>
        /// Clean up any resources being used.
        /// </summary>
        /// <param name="disposing">true if managed resources
should be disposed; otherwise, false.</param>
        protected override void Dispose(bool disposing)
        {
            if (disposing && (components != null))
            {
                components.Dispose();
            }
            base.Dispose(disposing);
        }

        #region Windows Form Designer generated code

        /// <summary>
        /// Required method for Designer support - do not modify
        /// the contents of this method with the code editor.
        /// </summary>
        private void InitializeComponent()
        {
            this.components = new
System.ComponentModel.Container();
            this.reportViewer1 = new
Microsoft.Reporting.WinForms.ReportViewer();
            this.SuspendLayout();
            //
            // reportViewer1
            //
            this.reportViewer1.Dock =
System.Windows.Forms.DockStyle.Fill;
            this.reportViewer1.Location = new
System.Drawing.Point(0, 0);
            this.reportViewer1.Name = "ReportViewer";
            this.reportViewer1.Size = new
System.Drawing.Size(800, 450);
            this.reportViewer1.TabIndex = 0;
            //
            // Form1
            //
            this.AutoScaleDimensions = new
System.Drawing.SizeF(8F, 16F);
            this.AutoScaleMode =
System.Windows.Forms.AutoScaleMode.Font;
```

```
            this.ClientSize = new System.Drawing.Size(800, 450);
            this.Controls.Add(this.reportViewer1);
            this.Name = "Form1";
            this.Text = "Form1";
            this.ResumeLayout(false);

        }

        #endregion

        private Microsoft.Reporting.WinForms.ReportViewer
reportViewer1;
    }
}
```

Once these are added to this section, if you go back over to the designer view of the form you will see:

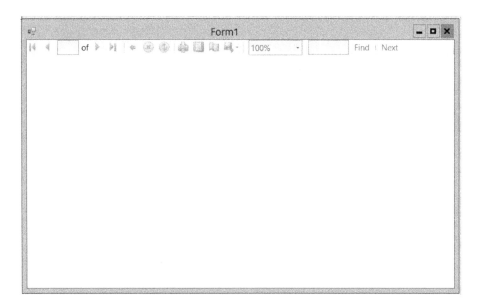

Now, we add the code in the form load to make all of this work together:

```
System.Data.DataSet ds = new System.Data.DataSet();

ds.ReadXml("C:\\Users\\Administrator\\source\\repos\\WindowsForms
App5\\WindowsFormsApp5\\CurrentVersion.xml");
```

```
reportViewer1.LocalReport.ReportPath =
"C:\\Users\\Administrator\\source\\repos\\WindowsFormsApp5\\Windo
wsFormsApp5\\Report2.rdlc";
reportViewer1.LocalReport.DataSources.Clear();
reportViewer1.LocalReport.DataSources.Add(new
Microsoft.Reporting.WinForms.ReportDataSource("DataSet1",
ds.Tables[0]));
reportViewer1.RefreshReport();
```

And when the application runs:

Name	Type	Data
BuildGUID	REG_SZ	ffffffff-ffff-ffff-ffff-ffffffffffff
BuildLab	REG_SZ	9600.winblue_ltsb.200225-0600
BuildLabEx	REG_SZ	9600.19665.amd64fre.winblue_ltsb.200225-0600
CurrentBuild	REG_SZ	9600
CurrentBuildNumber	REG_SZ	9600
CurrentType	REG_SZ	Multiprocessor Free
CurrentVersion	REG_SZ	6.3
EditionID	REG_SZ	ServerDatacenterEval
InstallationType	REG_SZ	Server
InstallDate	REG_DWORD	0x00000000 (0)
PathName	REG_SZ	C:\Windows
ProductName	REG_SZ	Windows Server 2012 R2 Datacenter Evaluation
RegisteredOrganization	REG_SZ	
RegisteredOwner	REG_SZ	Windows User
SoftwareType	REG_SZ	System
SystemRoot	REG_SZ	C:\Windows

Form2

1 of 1   100%   Find | Next

IN CONCLUSION

We've covered a lot of material

The code I have provided you will help you create reports in Visual Studio. What you do and where you go from here is entirely up to you.

Just remember that these kinds of reports require Visual Studio and cannot be run as independent reports without it.

In the next book, I'm going to be covering creating reports using html and HTA. Included in that book will be information on using CSS or Cascading Style Sheets to enhance the HTML and HTA visuals.

I'm sure that you will have noticed that this book didn't cover graphics. Things like charts and drawings can be combined with the reports but I thought this book should cover just working with and creating the reports. So, I left that out.

There is also the web version of the report viewer that I may consider creating a book on it as well.

With that said, good luck with your career and keep safe.

www.ingramcontent.com/pod-product-compliance
Lightning Source LLC
LaVergne TN
LVHW041214050326
832903LV00021B/619